NEWARK AND SHERWOOD RAMBLES

Malcolm McKenzie

SIGMA LEISURE

Wilmslow, England

First published in 1991 by Sigma Leisure - an imprint of Sigma Press, 1 South Oak Lane, Wilmslow, Cheshire SK9 6AR, England.

Whilst every effort has been made to ensure that the information given in this book is correct, neither the publisher nor the author accept any responsibility for any inaccuracy.

British Library Cataloguing in Publication Data
A CIP record for this book is available from the British Library.

ISBN: 1-85058-256-4

Typesetting and design by
Sigma Hi-Tech Services Ltd, Wilmslow

Printed and bound by
Manchester Free Press, Paragon Mill, Jersey St., Manchester M4 6FP.

Cover Picture: Walking near Edwinstowe, in Sherwood Forest.

Acknowledgements: The author would like to thank –

❏ Anne McKenzie, proof reader, walks-tester, and photographer.

❏ Des Whicher, for support and encouragement.

❏ Nottinghamshire County Council's Rights of Way section for blazing the trails.

❏ The members of Newark Ramblers for their companionship during twenty years of exploration.

Foreword

I have great pleasure in commending this book of walks in Newark and Sherwood District. Its author, Malcolm McKenzie, knows his subject superbly well.

I first came to Newark nearly 20 years ago and was soon walking on a regular basis with the Newark Group of Ramblers. This enabled me to get to know the local footpaths and to realise what good walking country there was in Nottinghamshire. Many of these walks have been included in this book and will enable others to enjoy the real delights that await those who explore on foot, the countryside in Newark and Sherwood.

When I first took over as Chairman of Newark and Sherwood District Council in May 1990, I hoped that it would be possible to do something to promote walking in my District. This the book does superbly well. The footpaths of the area are a superb heritage which must not be lost. The work of the Ramblers Association and of people like Malcolm is absolutely essential. This book will, I am sure, put more feet on the ground - the best safeguard there could be for the future of the footpath network.

Happy Walking!

Des Whicher – Chairman, Newark and Sherwood District Council

Location Map

Contents

INTRODUCTION

Mention Nottinghamshire and immediately a vision is conjured up of a rascally sheriff and gluttonous abbots bravely foiled or robbed by Robin Hood, Little John, Will Scarlet and Co.

Much of the Greenwood where these deeds were, or may have been done is now in the District of Newark and Sherwood, which comprises about a third of the County of Nottinghamshire.

The traveller moving from West to East across the County should have no difficulty in recognising three distinct North-South stripes. Geologically speaking, these correspond to Bunter sandstones, Keuper marl and alluvial sand and gravel. For the walker, there is simply a change in the character of the countryside.

First comes the Sherwood Forest area, which even in the Middle Ages was not just a sea of trees, but a patchwork of woodland with rough heath, glades, and cultivated plots which grew larger as time went on, basically a place for the King to hunt in. A few ragged walls of darkened stone at Clipstone are called King John's Palace: this was a hunting lodge for John and monarchs before and after him. Later, monastic foundations like Rufford carved estates in the forest, and post-Reformation nabobs who profited by the Nationalisation of the church developed the land even more. Later still deep mines exploited the seams of coal which lie beneath the forest. They left scars, many of which are greening over, planted with grass, then trees again, but some headstocks still rise rather incongruously out of their screen of forest.

Over the Hills

The second band of countryside consists of gently rolling uplands, a little heavier underfoot but more varied and still well-wooded. Small streams run from West to East, all bound for the river Trent. Where the stream gouges a deep valley for itself, it is known as a dumble. There is no coal here, but oil is extracted in commercial quantities, with the quiet farming village of Eakring the home to BP's local headquarters. Fortunately, oil-wells are much more discreet than coal-mines, and the occasional "nodding donkey" pump is an attraction rather than an eyesore.

Silver Trent

Finally, the Trent valley sweeps majestically through the eastern marches. The river banks are lined with charming villages, some displaying mementoes of the commercial river traffic which was once so important. At Newark, British Waterways have a repair yard right beside Town Lock and almost under the walls of the castle, and warehouses, now converted to landlubbers' purposes, line the canal basin.

The Trent valley is good farmland, producing barley for the breweries and sugar beet for the gargantuan factory only a mile from Newark, as well as wheat and oil-seed rape. Along much of the river banks, cattle or sheep graze the water-meadows, and flood-banks following the old tow-paths are a pleasure to walk.

The Trent valley is also a good source of sand and gravel, very necessary minerals whose extraction nevertheless causes a fair amount of aggravation to the neighbours. It also produces a number of holes in the ground, destined to be boating lakes or nature reserves after twenty years or so. East of the Trent the land remains fairly flat to the Nottinghamshire-Lincolnshire border, and from the gentle hills bordering the valley Lincoln Cathedral can often be seen perched above its town.

Towns

Newark may be the "capital" of its District, and one of the finest market towns in the land, but the spiritual centre must be Southwell, dominated by its Norman Minster. To the North, Ollerton grew in the last century into a prosperous mining town, but is still surrounded by quiet countryside. In fact, quiet countryside describes most of the area, and each village has its own charm and its own history. Churches are often the focal point of the village and the repository of records of past generations, but the pub, the manor house, the old smithy and the farm have a story to tell too. So have the water mills which still straddle many of the Trent's tributary streams, and the windmills converted to homes or standing eyeless and derelict.

Paths

There are upwards of fifteen hundred footpaths and bridleways between the Trent and Sherwood Forest. Their age varies, from the ridge-paths used long before the Romans came, to the field paths walked by villagers on their way to work, church or the inn. The 1949 National Parks and Access to the Countryside Act ensured that they were all recorded and maintained for the enjoyment of all walkers – and horse riders, in the case of bridleways – for pleasure and the benefits that fresh air and exercise bring. Paths were always there for a purpose, and many form a link between adjoining villages. A few of these links joined together, and you have a circular walk!

Literature

As walking has become more and more popular in recent years, books and leaflets have appeared describing walks in Nottinghamshire. The County Council's first publication of a book of fourteen walks in the mid-seventies was a success on a scale which surprised even the Rights of Way staff who had produced it, and a second book followed which is still available.

Later, separate leaflets were published of the same walks with additions, and copies of these too are still available. Together with some new leaflets produced in 1989, over fifty walks leaflets have been published by the County Council, sixteen describing walks in Newark and Sherwood district.

Long Distance Paths

There are now two long distance paths in Nottinghamshire, the Robin Hood Way and the Trent Valley Way. The former was produced by the Nottingham Wayfarers Rambling Club to link places connected with the legend of Robin Hood, and runs sinuously from Nottingham to Edwinstowe, a total of 88 miles. The prime mover of the path, which is described in an excellent book, was Chris Thompson, who can supply a copy if you write to him at 21 Spindle View, Calverton, Notts. The second long distance path was published by the County Council in 1989. A book describing the Trent Valley Way, a route wandering from Thrumpton to West Stockwith and never far from the Trent itself, is accompanied by a book of nine circular walks based on the longer route. These and the leaflets mentioned above are available from the Rights-of-Way Officer, Trent Bridge House, Fox Road, West Bridgford, Notts.

The Walks

This book offers thirty country walks, which have been written over a period of twenty years. It is twenty years since the formation of the Newark group of the Ramblers' Association, and as a founder member and sometime chairman and footpath secretary I have had twenty years of pleasurable exploration of the countryside round about. The members, as cheerful and companionable a bunch of people as you could hope to meet, have thoroughly tested all these walks, plus many others which have gone into the discard pile.

As Newark itself is a very special town, it has had to have a walk of its own. This is a Town Trail which skims the surface of Newark's history and traditions, and provides a pleasant stroll too.

Whither Shall I Wander?

Though some walkers like to cover as much ground as possible, this is certainly not a priority for most of the Ramblers I know, who like to take their time and occasionally "stand and stare". The times suggested for completing the walks allow for some leaning on a gate to look at the view, and perhaps a half-pint at one of our village pubs. Most of my walks are between four and eight miles long, though there is a ten-miler which had to be included simply because it's a superb walk.

All the walks are circular, which is important as public transport is patchy in many areas. Some walks are difficult to reach, and on Sundays there is little public transport to anywhere. None of the walks involves really steep climbing. Many of the paths are not only signposted, but have been waymarked along the route by County Council staff. The walks are numbered for easy pinpointing on the distribution map. They are numbered widdershins, or anti-clockwise, starting North of Newark and ending with number 31 in the town itself.

Pubs

Some tiny villages have a pub, while larger ones have none, so I have tried to name all those available. Nearly all those mentioned can provide lunch as well as a refreshing drink, and most walks can be timed to reach a pub for lunch half-way around.

Walkers tend to accumulate some of the countryside on their boots, and these are not therefore welcome to pub landlords, who are also resistant to the charms of bulky rucksacks and muddy dogs. All these could stay outside – in fine weather, there are usually seats and tables outside, anyway. Walkers who find removing their boots a tedious chore can carry two plastic bags to wear over them, thus not only keeping the landlord's carpets clean but giving the locals a laugh.

In spite of recent legislation, only pubs in tourist traps are liable to be open after three in the afternoon, and lunchtime opening on Sundays is still restricted to three hours in any case.

Parking

The walks usually start from some easily identifiable building, such as a church or pub. It is really vital, not just polite, to park so that no-one is obstructed, avoiding gateways and narrow lanes. Some pub landlords have kindly allowed walkers to use their car park, but please park as far from the pub itself as possible. It would be a nice gesture to have a drink after your walk and thank the landlord nicely!

Travel

Most of the walks can be reached by public transport, though some villages like Eakring, Ossington and Harby may only have one bus on market days. On Sunday, when most people are free to go walking, there are usually no buses at all. For walks accessible by train on the Nottingham to Lincoln line – those involving Collingham, Newark, Rolleston, Fiskerton, Bleasby, Thurgarton and Lowdham – there is a very good Monday to Saturday service, but only rare trains on Sundays starting about mid-day.

I have tried to indicate how easy it is to reach each venue by public transport, but it is always best to check. Since deregulation of bus services, these can change at short notice, though most rural services are run on contract to the County Council and rarely change. For up to date information, telephone Nottinghamshire's "buses hotline" on Nottingham (0602) 824264 or 824267 (Monday to Friday 8.30am to 5.00pm). Railway information is obtainable from Newark (0636) 704491 or Derby (0332) 32051.

Maps

I hope that the walk descriptions, together with my sketch maps, will provide enough information for accurate navigation. Of course it is always useful to have an Ordnance Survey map as well. The only practical map for checking a route is the Pathfinder 1:25,000 scale map (2.5 inches to the mile), which shows field boundaries and quite small details of the landscape. The map required is shown above each walk. To find the start of the walk, the Landranger 1:50,000 will do. Two of these cover most of the area, Sheet 120 Mansfield and the Dukeries and 129 Nottingham and Loughborough, but a few walks in the East are on Sheet 121 Lincoln.

Getting There

The start of each walk is given as a map reference, a six figure number preceded by the letters SK which designate the area covered by all these walks. If memories of longitude and latitude are a little hazy, proceed as follows:-

Look along the top edge of your map for the first two figures of the map reference. When you've found them, imagine the space between this number and the next divided into ten. The third figure of the map reference tells you how many tenths to measure along. From this point, imagine a line going down the map.

Next, look for the fourth and fifth figures on the edge of the map, use the sixth figure to measure tenths again, and imagine a line running from there across the map.

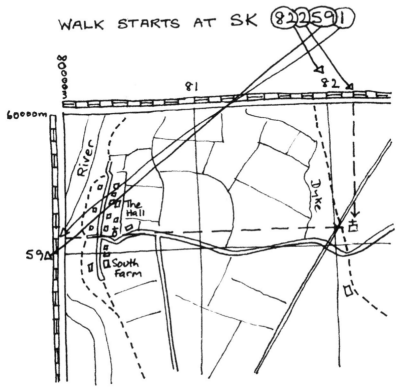

Where the two lines meet is where you want to be.

Be Prepared

When out walking it's always wise to carry a few essentials in a light rucksack. Even on the most perfect of days the weather can change, and waterproofs are the first necessity. Something to eat and drink could come in handy: fruit is the easiest food to carry, especially in dried form, and fizzy or alcoholic drinks are not as good for the thirst as fruit juice. A small first aid kit should always be carried, with at the least some sticking plasters, some bandage and ointment for scratches. You're unlikely to need a compass in this area, though many experienced walkers never go without one. Finally, if you forget to carry a camera you could regret it!

Miracles Take Longer

Over the last two decades, as walking has become increasingly popular, Nottinghamshire County Council's rights of way section has expanded in response to pressure from walkers to improve footpaths and bridleways. Certainly you are unlikely to find a stile or footbridge missing as you follow these walks, except for wear and tear, and problems are tackled as they arise. The difficult one to solve has been the illegal ploughing or cropping of footpaths in arable fields, but here there is hope after the passing of the Rights of Way Act 1990, which both clarifies the law on ploughing of rights of way and makes it easier for Local Authorities to deal with landowners who break the law. Briefly, headland paths – those which follow a field boundary – can not be ploughed and must be 1.5 metres wide if just a path and 3 metres if a bridleway. Cross-field paths may be ploughed, but should be clearly marked and made fit to walk on within 24 hours. They should be one metre wide, or 1.5 metres in the case of bridleways.

If crops are planted on the path and become an obstruction, Local Authorities have the right to remove the obstruction if the landowner will not, and send him the bill.

I have walked all the routes described in this book during the last year, and in a few cases have reported problems found to the County Council. Any serious obstructions reported to them are dealt with, and any walker who reports such obstructions has earned the gratitude of the rest of us! The person to write to is the Rights of Way Officer, Trent Bridge House, Fox Road, West Bridgford, Notts NG2 6BJ.

Country Code

We must never forget that people earn their living from the countryside, a tough enough job without problems caused by visitors. The Country Code is a set of rules which may seem common sense, but bear repeating here:

❏ Guard against all risk of fires

❏ Fasten all gates

❏ Keep dogs under proper control

❏ Keep to the paths across farmland

❏ Leave no litter

❏ Avoid damaging fences, hedges and walls

❏ Safeguard water supplies

❏ Protect wildlife, wild plants and trees

❏ Go carefully on country roads

❏ Respect the life of the countryside

Welcome to our World

It is a great pleasure to follow a few lines on a map and discover a beautiful walk through meadows and woodland, by rivers and streams, tracing ancient routes from village to village. An even greater pleasure is to share that walk with friends, so that they can enjoy it too.

I hope you enjoy these walks, and if you would like to enjoy more, join a walking group. My local group is part of the Ramblers' Association, whose National office is at 1/5 Wandsworth Road, London SW8 2XX.

Happy Rambling!

1: COLLINGHAM

A gentle stroll in the Trent Valley which mainly circles around the large village of Collingham.

Distance: 3.75 miles

Time: 1.5 hours

Start: Grey Horse Inn, North Collingham, map reference SK 832625

Map: Pathfinder SK 86/96 (Lincoln South), Landranger 121 (Lincoln)

How to Get There:

By Car: Take A46 and A1133 from Newark

By Bus: There are regular services from Newark.

By Train: Collingham has a station on the Nottingham to Lincoln line. Walkers arriving by rail can join the walk on Station Road.

Refreshments: Grey Horse

Nearest Tourist Information: The Ossington, Beastmarket Hill, Newark (opposite the castle) Tel 0636 78962

Until relatively recently a large village with High and Low Streets and some ribbon development on side streets, Collingham has grown into a small town serving many little villages around it. It has succeeded nine times in winning the Best Kept Village trophy in its class, and has produced a Village Trail, which is available in local shops.

Starting the walk at the Grey Horse Inn, cross the main road and turn right into the village until you are opposite the Cross. Keep left past the phone box to enter a narrow ginnel with a fence left and hedge right. The clear path crosses three small fields and continues as a fenced ginnel to Swinderby Road. Cross the road and follow another ginnel, then continue past the football pitches and bowling green of Collingham Football Club to Station Road.

Take the path straight ahead through a tunnel of garden hedges and across a field to a stile. Enter The Paddock, a short street of modern houses leading to Dyke's End. Cross this street half-right to pass between a house and a garage and cross the stile.

In the large field, removal of hedges have made the line of the path fairly meaningless, but go ahead, passing a stile left, until level with a handgate to the railway left. Turn right to follow the left-hand edge of the field and reach the road opposite the cricket field.

Cross the road carefully, enter the gate of the cricket field, and keep to the right-hand side, continuing along a narrow ginnel to Cottage Lane. Cross this and go straight on to the next street, South End, where you turn left to the end. Cross the fence and turn right to reach the Fleet, a tiny stream which, it is said, follows the old course of the Trent. Cross and turn half-right to a gap, then straight across the next field to where a gate gives access to a short track leading to Westfield Lane.

This is the correct path, though it is clear that local walkers keep around the right-hand edges of the two fields. Turn left along the lane, passing Westfield Farm which is usually guarded by a flock of geese. Go on till you find a short lane on the right, which you follow to the end. Walk along the hedge on your right to Carlton Ferry Lane.

Turn right, then left along a grassy lane 200 yards further on. Where this joins Northcroft Lane, go straight ahead until a signpost on your left points cross-field to the Fleet. Cross the footbridge and turn right, angling across the long meadow towards the far hedge. Cross the bridge and gate at the end of the meadow and continue left to a ginnel leading into Low Street. Turn left to return to the Grey Horse.

2: *CARLTON-ON-TRENT*

An easy walk beside the river Trent and along quiet lanes, between two lovely villages you will want to explore.

Distance: 4 miles

Time: 2 hours

Start: Carlton-on-Trent church, map reference SK 799639

Maps: Pathfinder SK 66/76 (Ollerton) and 86/96 (Lincoln South), Landranger 120 (Mansfield and the Dukeries)

How to Get There:

By Car: Carlton-on-Trent is 6.5 miles North of Newark and just off the A1.

By Bus: Services are about once an hour from Newark or Retford. None on Sundays.

Refreshments: Lord Nelson, Sutton-on-Trent, Great Northern, Carlton-on-Trent

Nearest Tourist Information: The Ossington, Beastmarket Hill, Newark, Tel 0636 78962

Carlton is a delightful village, now peacefully by-passed by the A1. Its most imposing building is the late Georgian Hall, behind its high walls and iron gates, home of the Vere-Laurie family. The Dower House is opposite and the Victorian church nearby. However my favourite building is the old blacksmith's shop just a short stroll south down the village street. It bears a huge horseshoe in decorative brickwork and the message:-

"Gentlemen as you pass by, Upon this shoe please cast your eye, If it be too strait I'll make it wider, I'll ease the horse and please the rider, If lame from shoeing as they often are, You may have them eased with The Greatest Care."

Starting at the church, walk North out of the village, passing on your left Carlton Hall. Turn right and go past attractive cottages towards the Mill. As you pass close to the river there is little sign that this was once a busy wharf. The mill has the largest tower in the county, but is now disused.

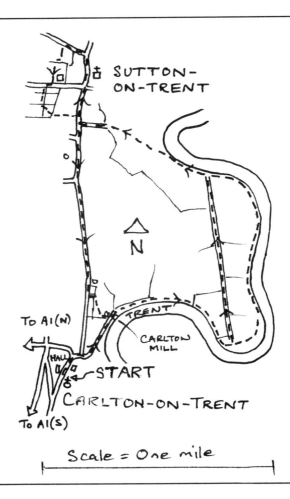

Walk past the mill and go through a gate. Cross a stile beside a flood-bank left (also a footpath), pass through the next gateway, and after crossing the next fence follow the flood-bank sharp left, then left again to cross a stile and enter an old green lane leading north.

(Alternatively, you can continue to follow the river). The lane cuts off a loop in the river, and on reaching the river bank you turn left through a gate.

Follow the track which swings left towards Sutton-on-Trent, joining Far Holme Lane. Turn right to pass the church, bearing left after the school along Bulham Lane. About 100 yards on the left is a footbridge and stile. Go straight through the tree nursery, then right to a gap. Pass through and follow the track to emerge in the Old England car park. Go on to the road. Turn right and immediately left down a narrow ginnel, over the stile at the end, across a small meadow to a stile, and diagonally left on a well-used path and down another ginnel to High Street.

Turn right and go through the village, passing the Lord Nelson on your left. Ignore the right hand bend and continue ahead along Carlton Lane. Crossing a little bridge where bollards prevent through traffic, pass houses and take the narrow path on your left between high hedges. Cross the stile at the end and angle right to another stile in the corner of the field. Cross an attractive garden to join the lane near Carlton Mill, and turn right to return to the church.

The Blacksmith's Shop, Carlton-on-Trent

3: SUTTON-ON-TRENT and GRASSTHORPE

Once on the main route from London to Newcastle, Sutton-on-Trent is still a substantial Trent-side village, with an imposing hotel and two other hostelries, shops and a library. By contrast, Grassthorpe is just a scatter of pleasant houses on a double bend, but it has its own charm.

Distance: 5 miles

Time: 2 hours

Start: Sutton-on-Trent church, map reference SK 800659

Maps: Pathfinders SK66/76 (Ollerton) and 86/96 (Lincoln South), Landrangers 120 (Mansfield & the Dukeries) and 121 (Lincoln)

How to Get There:

By Car: By the A1 from Newark, turning off at Carlton-on-Trent

By Bus: Regular services from Newark and Retford, but not on Sundays

Refreshments: There are an hotel and two pubs in Sutton-on-Trent

Nearest Tourist Information: The Ossington, Beastmarket Hill, Newark, Tel 0636 78962

Start at the impressive church of All Saints. Once it stood taller, as it had a spire until 1830. The most impressive part of the church is the ornate Mering Chapel, built to shelter the tomb of a local grandee.

From the church, walk south to the nearby junction with High Street on your right, which you follow as far as the Old England Hotel. Turn right past the hotel and a home with neat garden just beyond, following a wide grass path to a tree nursery. Angle a couple of yards right: a path between the saplings brings you to a footbridge and Bulham Lane.

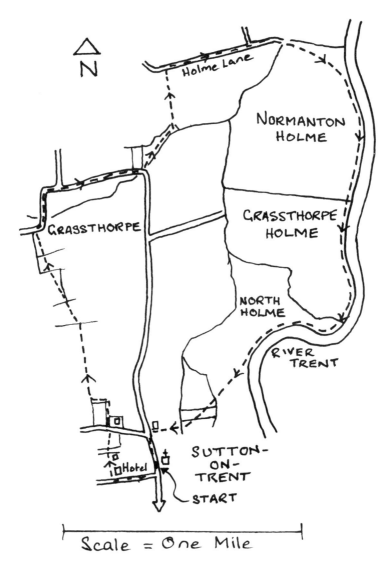

At the time of writing a footpath diversion is being sought, which will mean we have only to cross the lane half-left and walk north beside the hedge. The path then turns left, still by the hedge, to join a farm track, and right to go straight ahead to a footbridge.

Angle slightly left to a stile, then head slightly left again, across the meadow to a gate. Keep along the left-hand edges of two small meadows, then cross the stile to the left of the gate to reach the road. Continue straight ahead along Town Street: go round the right-hand bend, but do not swing left at the next bend. Keep straight on along Ingram Lane for about half a mile, and just before the white-railed bridge cross the fence left. Follow the stream to the end of the meadow, pass through the gate and turn sharp left to the signposted gate.

Turn right along Holme Lane, go over the stiles at the end and go on to the riverside. The riverside grazing land belonging to the villages of Normanton, Grassthorpe and Sutton, known as Holmes, are in fact commons over which there are local rights of grazing.

Turn right along the floodbank. After crossing a narrow bridge to Grassthorpe Holme, then a wider one to Sutton North Holme, follow the floodbank until it swings left. Now head right for Sutton church. Cross a stile and angle half-left to another. Cross the next meadow diagonally right to a stile near the corner. Now cut across the corner of the next field to a footbridge, and after crossing the floodbank go straight ahead beside the concrete flood-wall to reach the road. Turn left to return to the church.

4: GIRTON & SOUTH CLIFTON

Riverside paths and an old Green Lane link these two Trent Valley villages, each a pleasure to visit. Gravel workings are part of the scene, but for boating enthusiasts, the lakes they leave behind are good news.

Distance: 6.5 miles

Time: 3 hours

Start: Girton Church, map reference SK 826663

Maps: Pathfinder SK 86/96 (Lincoln South), Landranger 121 (Lincoln)

How to Get There:

By Car: Girton is just off the A1133 on the Newark to Gainsborough road

By Bus: Reasonable services from Newark

Refreshments: Red Lion, South Clifton

Nearest Tourist Information: The Ossington, Beastmarket Hill, Newark (opposite the castle) Tel 0636 78962

The walk starts at Girton church, where there is room for only one or two cars, so bigger groups please park outside the village's narrow lanes. Go down West Lane opposite, keeping right at the end and crossing the stile left after a few yards. Follow the top of the floodbank across three grass fields, then drop down to a stile. Ignoring the inviting footpath sign on your left, cross the tree-lined lane. The path continues along the floodbank at the edge of two fields, then on to the Trent, near its confluence with the river Fleet. Across the river, Sutton-on-Trent church can be seen among trees. Keep to the floodbank beside the river Trent, using the steps provided to cross two conveyor belts used by the sand and gravel company to transport its wares to the wharf. Continue for a mile and a half, with the giant cooling towers of Marnham power station ahead as the river twists and turns. Watch out for the flock of Canada geese who normally graze this stretch. Cross a bridge and two

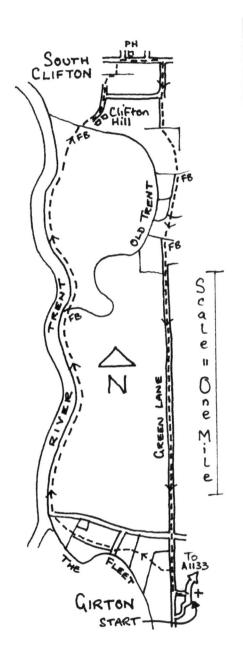

stiles and pass through the gate by Cliftonhill Farm, joining the lane which leads into South Clifton.

When the lane bends sharp right, walkers who need no refreshment can by-pass South Clifton: pass the sports field and, when the road turns sharp left, take the track on the right instead which leads up to the lofty eminence of Clifton Hill (76 feet above sea level).

Alternatively, go straight ahead at the first (right-hand) bend along a lane shaded by large ash trees, through a white gate and go round the corner of the sports field. Past the goal-posts is a narrow ginnel leading to the village street opposite the Red Lion. After a refreshing drink, keep right along the village street and right again at the first turn-ing towards Clifton Hill. You are now following the Trent Valley Way.

In the field at the top of the hill, angle left to pass close to a telegraph pole and walk along the floodbank ahead. A concrete bridge takes you over a stream, then follow the right-hand edge of the field. Near the corner is a section of wooden fence and a stile, then you head straight across the next field towards the nearest pylon.

Cross the plank bridge, then keep along the right-hand edge of the next field to reach a lane. Follow this for a mile and a half to return to Girton, passing worked-out gravel pits which are now used by Hoveringham Sailing Club.

5: HARBY & DODDINGTON

A walk on the borders of Nottinghamshire and Lincolnshire with a variety of woodlands and a Stately Home.

Distance: 6.5 miles

Time: 3 hours

Start: Bottle & Glass, Harby, map reference SK 880708

Maps: Pathfinder SK 87/97 (Lincoln and Saxilby), Landranger 121 (Lincoln)

How to Get There:

By Car: From Lincoln, via the A57, leaving it at Saxilby, and from Newark, on the A1133, turning off at Besthorpe.

By Bus: Forget it

Nearest Tourist Office: 21, The Cornhill, Lincoln, Tel 0522 512971

Harby is Nottinghamshire's easternmost parish in a salient thrust into Lincolnshire. A notice-board near the church explains that Queen Eleanor, beloved wife of Edward 1, died at the manor house here in 1290. Her body was conveyed to Westminster Abbey for burial, and wherever it lay en route Edward erected a cross, the best known being Charing Cross.

From the Bottle & Glass, walk south along High Street and where it bends right keep straight ahead along Church Street. After a few yards fork left along a grassy track waymarked as a bridleway. On your left is a fenced paddock, usually home to a few sheep, while a children's play-park can be seen on the right with a bowling-green beyond. Turn left just before the ditch, with the fence on your left. Follow the ditch, first with no field boundary, then with a hedge on your right. In the next field, the well-used path is around the right-hand edge to a gate. A few yards further on is a gate on your right, where you leave the bridleway

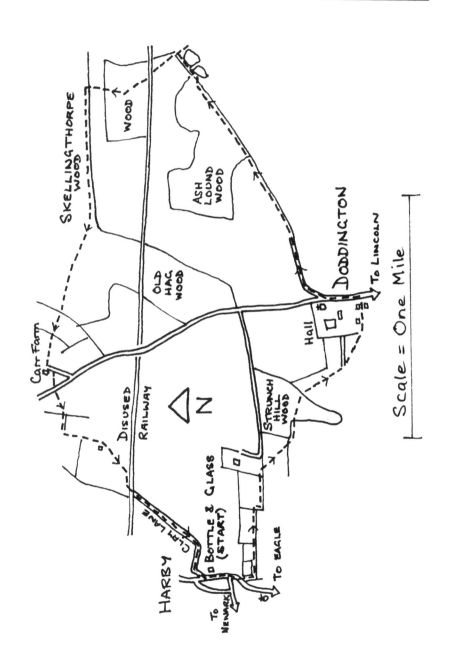

to head for Doddington Hall. After passing through the gate, head half-left to a handgate near the far corner of the field, beside an electricity post. Go through and turn left along the woodside, go through a gap in the blackthorn hedge and pass through a small glade. The hall can be seen across an arable field, but we reach it by a roundabout route. Firstly, turn right across a piece of wetland marked out as a nature trail, where meadowsweet and salad burnet can be found: you will find a stile at the other side.

Doddington Hall

Continue to the end of a line of poplars and on to pass just right of a building: the path is always beautifully maintained through the crops. Continue left along a track and through farm buildings to a road. Turn left in Doddington to pass in front of Doddington Hall. If you can arrange to do the walk on a summer Wednesday, Sunday or Bank Holiday Monday the hall will be open.

The hall was designed by Robert Smithson, who started his career at Longleat. It is a distinguished Elizabethan mansion which thankfully has seen little change since it was built in 1600, though some of its outbuildings have become private houses. It is the family home of the Jarvis family, whose care of the house and gardens extends to the rights of way around it.

Carry on past the church and cross the road to enter a lane. This swings right and continues first as a surfaced road, then as a track to Ash Lound Wood and along a ride that follows its edge. A narrow path now winds through a scattering of oaks and eventually angles right to pass a settling-pond and a fishing-lake with a small wild-fowl population. At a T-junction at the end of the lake, turn left through a gate and along the edge of a meadow to a disused railway. Go a few yards left along this track, then right into a wood of oak and ash standards on a clear path: this can get muddy after rain. This leads to a track which you follow to a T-junction. Here turn left and follow the path through Skellingthorpe Wood, first past oak and ash, then pine plantations with self-sown hazel and field maple, then lime. Where the clear path swings right, continue ahead on a grassy ride which ends at a ditch and stile.

Cross the stile and cross the field to a gap. Continue to Carr Farm, turn left through the gates, then right across the field to a gate. Cross the road to the gate opposite and on across the field to a gateway. Continue with the hedge on your left to a track and turn left through a gate. Continue to a pylon, then head 45 degrees right across the field which should bring you to what was a level crossing. Cross the remnants of the track and follow Clay Lane into Harby. Keep left to return to the Bottle & Glass.

6: CAUNTON & NORWELL

A walk using mainly field paths linking two fine villages and skirting a third, Bathley

Distance: 6 miles

Time: 3 hours

Start: Caunton church, map reference SK 745601

Maps: Pathfinder SK 65/75 (Newark-on-Trent West) and SK 66/76 (Ollerton), Landranger 120 (Mansfield and the Dukeries)

How to Get There:

By Car: Caunton is 6 miles NW of Newark, just off the A616 Ollerton road.

By Bus: There is a reasonable bus service from Newark, but NOT on Sundays.

Refreshments: The pubs at Caunton and Norwell are both "The Plough", and both provide drinks and snacks.

Nearest Tourist Information: The Ossington, Beastmarket Hill, Newark (opposite the Castle) Tel 0636 78962.

Caunton, a village of 400 or so inhabitants, is a pleasant place to live. It has a mediaeval church, a pub, and a school, as well as a Manor, a Grange, a windmill and a Beck complete with ducks. With practical wisdom the villagers reject a modern sewage system, as they know this encourages the dreaded Developers. Fortunately, they also keep their footpaths in good order.

Starting at Caunton church, walk past the "Plough" and turn right along Norwell Road for a few yards. Church Farm on the right has the "trade mark" of Lord Middleton, an early landowner in the village: five courses of blue slates above the eaves. Go through the gate left and cross the paddock to a handgate, then continue to the right corner of the next

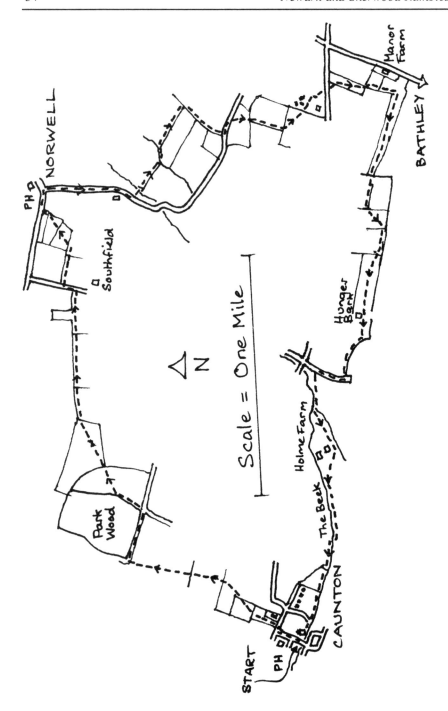

paddock. The handgate gives access to a large field, where you follow the same line. Passing through another gate, cross two arable fields, heading for the left-hand corner of Park Wood. Here you join a farm track, and turn right beside the wood. At the next corner, turn left beside the wood until you reach a ride through the wood. With your back to this, head slightly left to a gap in the hedge opposite indicating a footbridge.

Beyond is a large meadow which you cross corner to corner. Right of the corner is a plank bridge: after crossing, follow the edge of three fields to a road. Turn left for 150 yards, go through the farm gate and follow the edges of two ridge and furrow meadows. A few yards into the second, cross the stile left and pass through two small grass fields with a bridge mid-way. Now a short grassy lane leads to a road, where you turn right into Norwell. At a junction, you will find the "Plough" just to your left: our route is right along the Bathley road. Soon after passing a row of newly-renovated cottages, take the signposted stile left and cross a grass bridge. Go through the gate ahead and along the edge of the meadow to a footbridge over a stream. Here you should find a crop of teasels, a plant much favoured by flower arrangers.

Turn left along the farm track , but only around the corner, then go up the hill beside the hedge. At the top a rough farm track will be found: turn right to return to the road. Turn left here to walk along beside Fox Covert, and half way along turn right and take the track across it. You emerge beside the end of a hedge, which you keep on your right as you drop down to the stile beside an elderly willow.

Cross the meadow half-left to a stile. At this point you pass between farm buildings of Sunnybrook Farm and a long pool, following a line of hawthorns. Crossing a stile, turn right for a few yards, then cross stiles and a small paddock and slip right to reach the road.

Over the road, take the signposted path half-left to a stile. Now head up the long meadow to the far corner and a stile, then keep right behind a small farmhouse on the fringe of Bathley village. After crossing a stile turn right up a long, narrow meadow, clearly a relict of the mediaeval field system, and through the gate at the top. Follow the hedge ahead to a stile, then cross the next field to the left-hand corner. There is a gap in the hedge here, after which you follow the hedge up the hill to join a farm track. Go ahead along the track to pass just left of Hunger Barn. There is a fine panoramic view here with a wealth of woodland, Caunton almost hidden by trees ahead. Go straight on to join a field boundary, a grassy baulk with a scattering of blackthorn. Follow it downhill to the end of an ancient lane, largely taken over by hawthorn and elder. However if you turn right you will find a clear path winding through it: as you leave the wooded track, go through the gate on the left.

Go ahead to join the line of trees beside the Beck and follow it to a footbridge. After crossing this tributary of the Beck, turn left beside it. Pass through a gate, negotiate two stiles at either side of a farm track and angle right past the end of a barn and a lone ash tree to rejoin the Beck. Cross the tiny stream by another footbridge and turn left to follow it again. A new stile and bridge give access to a small paddock awash with daisies, which you cross and continue beside the stream along the foot of several gardens. Pass through the churchyard and you are back to base.

7: CAUNTON & NORWELL WOODHOUSE

A pleasant short walk from an attractive village, and with a high proportion of grass in this mainly arable area. All paths are well maintained.

Distance: 3.5 miles

Time: 1.5 hours

Start: Caunton church, map reference 745601

Map: Pathfinder SK 66/76 (Ollerton)

How to Get There:

By Car: Caunton is 6 miles NW of Newark, just off the A616 Ollerton Road.

By Bus: There is a reasonable bus service from Newark, but NOT on Sundays.

Refreshments: The "Plough", Caunton.

Nearest Tourist Information: The Ossington, Beastmarket Hill, Newark (opposite the Castle) Tel 0636 78962.

From Caunton Church, cross the bridge over the Beck and turn right along Manor Road. The Manor, set back from the road, was the home of Caunton's favourite son, Samuel Reynolds Hole, who became vicar of Caunton and later Dean of Rochester in 1887. A rose enthusiast who was the first President of the Rose Society, he was responsible for the renovation of the church in the 1860's and for the roses which still grow in its churchyard.

Turn right again along Ford Lane: the ford is no problem, a footbridge is provided! At the top swing left and follow the road round a right-hand bend and uphill past attractive cottages. Nearly straight ahead of you there is a stile beside an ancient willow: continue up the hill beside the hedge. Angle left as soon as possible to the corner of this ridge-and-furrow field. Cross a stile, then a second after a few yards along the edge of an arable field. Now continue the same line down a long

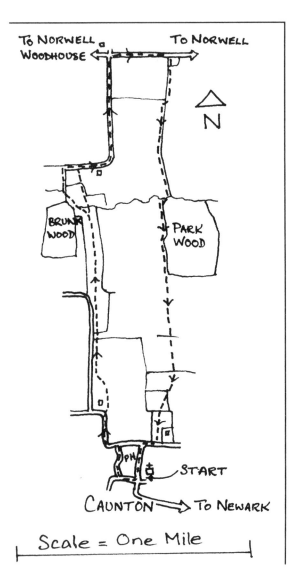

meadow. As you approach a small stream you may ford it and follow the bridleway straight ahead to a lane, but this could be tricky without wellies.

Alternatively, you can bear left as you approach the stream, cross the bridge in the corner, and go round the corner of the next field to another bridge. After crossing this, turn right to join the farm road.

In either case, turn right to follow the lane, passing Highfield House and its pheasant-pens. Turn right on reaching the road: after 300 yards go through the gate on the right near a ruined building, along the edge of the first field and part of the second.

Go through the gateway on your right, turning left immediately to follow the same line.

On reaching the wood, cross a bridge and pass through the corner of Park Wood. Turn left along the edge of the wood, an interesting deciduous wood with a fringe of ash trees. At the end Caunton comes into view: continue straight ahead to a footbridge, then on the same line to a gate. Cross the meadow, heading for the church. Pass through a handgate, continue to another, then cross the paddock to a road. Turn right, then left to return to the church.

8: OSSINGTON & MOORHOUSE

An appealing little walk from the village that time forgot.

Distance: 4 miles

Time: 2 hours

Start: Lay-by near the entrance to Ossington Hall gates, map reference SK 762648

How to Get There:

By Car: From the A1 or the A616 on the road between Carlton-on-Trent and Kneesall

By Bus: Impossible

Refreshments: Carry your own supplies

Nearest Tourist Office: The Ossington, Beastmarket Hill, Newark (opposite the castle) Tel 0636 78962

Starting from the newly-painted gates which once led to Ossington Hall, follow the road to the right past Hall Farm, but don't miss a building in the trees on the left. This 'classical' well, decorated with terra-cotta panels, is dedicated to Edward Denison, son of the Bishop of Salisbury, who died in 1870. The road bends sharp right, then passes Keeper's Cottage. Immediately afterwards, turn right behind the cottage and along the impressive Long Plantation, an overgrown avenue of mature oaks, sycamore and beech. Where this ends, keep left to rejoin the road then right for a few yards.

Turn left along a well-kept farm road, with the welcome sight of tree-planting on the right to replace the victims of Dutch Elm Disease. On reaching Cocked Hat Plantation on your left, follow the bridleway along the edge, then left beside a hedge to Wadnal Plantation. This wood, mainly oak trees, is usually home to a tribe of noisy rooks.

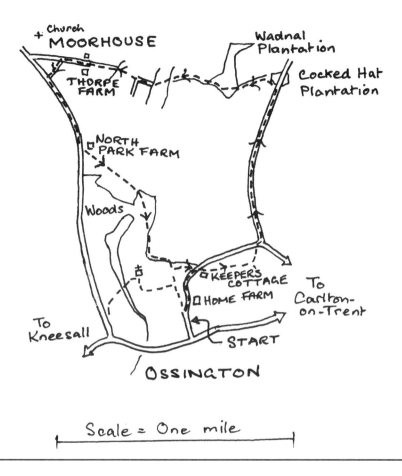

Cross the wood diagonally, then follow the route inside the wood. Cross the plank bridge and continue along the edge of two fields. Cross a farm bridge here and angle slightly left across an arable field to reach the end of an old lane marked by a scattering of ash trees. Follow the lane which produces swathes of meadowsweet and continue across arable to a gate and stile. The next field is grass: follow the edge to a stile beside Thorpe Farm and continue along the lane. The small community of Moorhouse can be seen to the right: it is now part of a larger parish, Laxton & Moorhouse.

Cross the stile on the left, follow the dyke to Ossington Road and turn left along it to North Park Farm. Enter the field on the left just beyond the farm and angle left across the field. There are no landmarks, but hopefully a path will be made through the crops to an earth bridge, then straight on to the corner of what was once the Ossington estate's sewage works. Wend your way across this now overgrown corner to reach a woodland track, where you turn left.

There is little sign on this pleasant tree-shaded track that Ossington Hall was once here: there is only a clearing on the right where it stood (it was demolished in 1963), and to the left the long-abandoned cricket field and parkland trees standing among arable crops. When the track swings right, take a narrow path past rusting reminders of the tennis-court to join the road opposite Keeper's Cottage. Turn right to return to your starting-point.

If you have some moments to spare, walk up the drive and left to the Church, which was built in the eighteenth century by John Carr of York, architect of Newark's Town Hall. It is at its best in Spring when the snowdrops and crocuses run riot in the churchyard.

9: LAXTON & KNEESALL

The village of Laxton in mid-Nottinghamshire is an agricultural fossil, still practicing the mediaeval open-field system. Green lanes and field-paths link it to the hilltop village of Kneesall.

Distance: 5 miles

Time: 2.5 hours

Start: Visitors Centre car park (behind the "Dovecote", map reference SK 724671)

Maps: Pathfinder SK 66/76 (Ollerton), Landranger 120 (Mansfield and the Dukeries)

How to Get There:

By Car: Laxton is best approached from the A616 Newark to Ollerton Road.

By Bus: There are buses every 2 hours between Tuxford and Ollerton.

Refreshments: The Dovecote, Laxton, The Angel, Kneesall

Nearest Tourist Office: The Ossington, Beastmarket Hill, Newark (opposite the castle) Tel 0636 78962

It might be useful to look into the Visitor Centre before setting off, as it will give more meaning to the landscapes you cross. Here is described the system of strip-farming which is still used. A leaflet describing a village trail is also available. From the Visitor Centre, go up to the church and turn along the short lane beside it. Slip left into the corner of the churchyard and go out by the handgate into the paddock behind. Cross the stile ahead and angle left down the hill to the corner, passing humps and hollows where once there were fish-ponds. Cross a bridge, then keep half-left across the arable field beyond to a stile in the corner.

In the road, turn away from Laxton: after 200 yards, a gap on the right leads into an old lane called Langsyke. Part of this used for access is

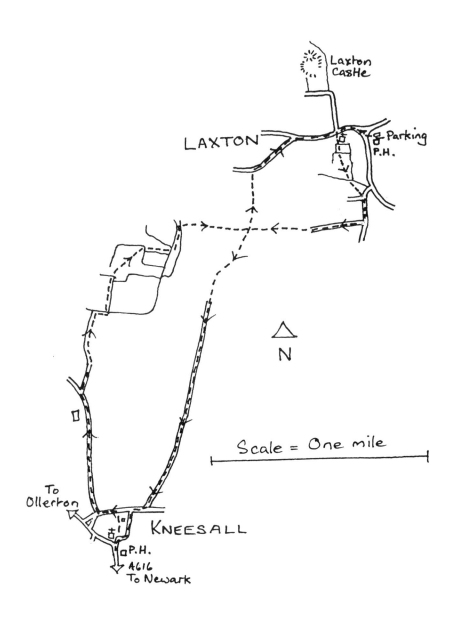

mown, the upper end, recently planted with a variety of trees, can become overgrown in summer. The lane brings you out on to Mill Field, which with West Field and South Field rotates its crops each year. Ignoring any side-tracks, go on to a crossroad and turn left down the hill on a well-used track. Ahead can be seen the hedged track which you are to follow to Kneesall. On reaching a road, turn right.

For refreshments, take the first left, School Lane, which brings you to the A616 beside the church, then turn left to the "Angel". On returning, enter School Lane and follow the footpath ahead along the edge of the school playing field, then turn left.

The route continues to the Green, where you turn right along Baulk Lane. Follow this quiet lane for about half a mile and turn right down a short lane past a pylon. When the track swings right, keep on down the left side of the field, then along the foot to a stile and bridge. Now go up the field with a hedge right and cross a stile in the corner.

Entering a large field, pass a lone tree and continue to the right-hand corner ahead. Pass through the hedge and turn right to a gap to reach the syke. This stretch of grassland, pronounced 'sik', is maintained alongside the Mill Field and elsewhere for hay. Bids are put in to harvest it each year.

Turn left for 200 yards and turn right along a row of bushes which bring you to a track. Ignore the track leading off left to the site of the long-vanished mill, marked by a small spinney, but go on to a crossroad. Turn left to reach a road, then turn right to walk through the village to your starting point.

A visit to Laxton is not complete without an excursion to the castle. Go up Hall Lane opposite the church, then cross the stile ahead. The humps and bumps in the castle bailey mark the site of the sixteenth century manor house whose stones have long since gone to form the basis of village farm houses. Beyond is a deep moat, then the mound of the motte.

10: WALESBY & KIRTON

The village of Walesby lies midway between the two Nottinghamshire coal mines of Ollerton and Bevercotes, and no more than two miles from each, but there is no sign of coal in this rural and forest walk.

Distance: 7 miles

Time: 3 hours

Start: Walesby Church, map reference SK 685707

Maps: Pathfinder SK 66/76 (Ollerton) and 67/77 (Clumber Park), Landranger 120 (Mansfield and the Dukeries)

How to Get There:

By Car: Walesby is on the B6387 just north of Ollerton

By Bus: There is an hourly service from Retford, Ollerton, or Mansfield. On Sundays, there is a two-hourly service from Mansfield only.

Refreshment: Red Lion, Walesby, Fox & Hounds, Kirton

Nearest Tourist Information: Ollerton Roundabout (SK 651675), Tel 0623 824545

Walesby lies in an area of mixed farming at the centre of a network of pleasant footpaths. Walesby Common, an area too poor for cultivation, is intensively used by the Scout movement, and the Forestry Commission woods to north and south of it, linked by an attractive bridleway, provide a favourite walk for the people of Ollerton and Boughton.

The walk starts at Walesby church. Go down the snicket to the right of the church, turn right along Manor Close, then left at the main street to pass the 'Red Lion'. Where the street bends right, follow the lane ahead until it rises and swings right: go through the gap left and head just left of Kirton church. After the second fence angle left to a footbridge. Go up the edge of the grass field to a gate, then half-right to a stile. Turn right and pass Kirton church, which dominates the village from its little wooded hill. Continue to the Fox and Hounds for refreshment.

Continue for a hundred yards, then take the signposted path right. Just beyond on the village street can be seen Hall Farm, one of the oldest buildings in Kirton, built by the Clarkson family in 1630. Go along the right-hand edge of the field, cross a stile right and follow the hedgerow to a bridge and stile. Angle slightly left to another stile, go along the hedged lane ahead to the end and cross the stiles left cutting off the

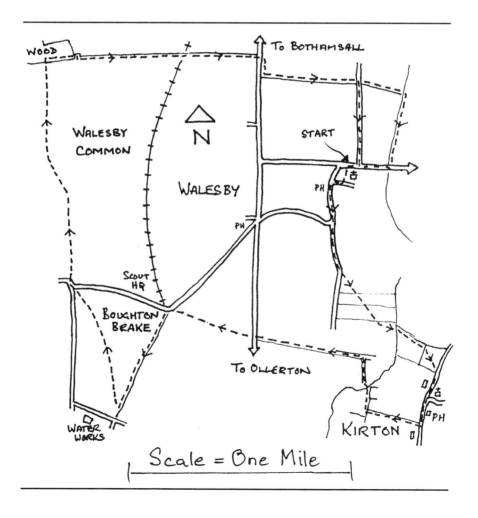

corner. Turn left along the lane and follow the fence to the road. Cross, follow the signposted path to a road and go on to the corner of Boughton Brake Wood, a plantation on the pebbly sand which typifies the rest of the walk. Turn left along the sandy path at the edge of the wood, and at the junction by the corner of the waterworks turn sharply right to go diagonally across the wood, keeping left at a fork. On leaving the wood, keep on across a double bend and follow the Bridleway sign. This route is known locally as the 'King's Road' and pre-dates the existing roads by several centuries.

The stream to the left is known at this point as Whitewater, but is also the river Maun. On its bank is a feature marked on the map as Robin Hood's Cave, but it would be little shelter for one Merry Man and is not worth a detour.

When this attractive path has crossed the Common and enters woodland, turn right immediately, and after a right turn swing left again. Follow the field edge, cross the mineral railway and edge left into a fenced path to reach the road.

Kirton Church

Cross the road, enter the field and keep right along two sides of it. On reaching a track, you can turn right along it to Walesby church. Alternatively, you can cross the track and follow the field edge to Bevercotes Beck. Cross the bridge, turn right along the bank to a road, crossing a stile on the way, and turn right to the church.

11: CLIPSTONE

An easy walk between Old and New Clipstone which is ideal for the winter months, as it follows only well-surfaced tracks or lanes.

Distance: 5.5 miles

Time: 2.5 hours

Start: Dog & Duck, Old Clipstone, map reference SK 606649

Maps: Pathfinder SK 46/56 (Mansfield North) and 66/76 (Ollerton), Landranger 120 (Mansfield and the Dukeries).

How to Get There:

By Car: via the B6030 from Mansfield

By Bus: There is an hourly service from Mansfield, Sundays included.

Refreshments: The Dog & Duck, Clipstone

Nearest Tourist Information: Ollerton Roundabout (SK 824545); Tel: 0623 824545

Start at the "Dog & Duck", Old Clipstone (SK 606649). The landlord asks his rambling customers to park at the bottom of the car park. Over the valley to the right you can see "King John's Palace", which was a royal hunting lodge from 1160 to about 1400. The ruin is a remnant of a lodge built for Edward 1 in 1280, some time after King John's death at Newark Castle.

Down the valley the twin headstocks of Clipstone pit show where New Clipstone grew up, some distance from the old village. Follow the track down the valley, with grass fields on the right and rough ground peppered with gorse left. Keep straight ahead to pass under three long tunnels built to carry railway tracks to the pit, though one is now a waggonway. Here you will find a small pond, then Vicar Pond, a fishing lake. The old spoil heaps here have ben grassed and planted with a wide variety of trees, turning an eyesore into a beauty spot. Turn right along

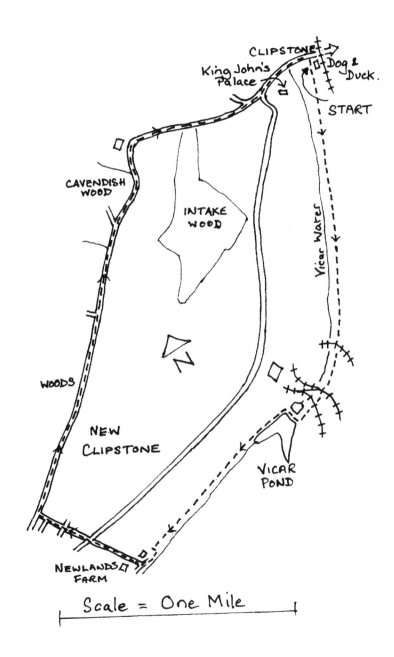

CLIPSTONE

King John's Palace

Dog & Duck.

START

CAVENDISH WOOD

INTAKE WOOD

Vicar Water

N

WOODS

NEW CLIPSTONE

VICAR POND

NEWLANDS FARM

Scale = One Mile

the track between the two ponds and follow it round Vicar Pond, then straight on, ignoring all side tracks until, after a mile, you have passed the long fence of "Bridleways". Turn right here to join the A611, cross and continue up Newlands Drive.

At the top, turn right following Clipstone Drive which soon becomes a hedged track, with woodland on your left. After passing Cavendish Lodge and its riding stables, the lane is surfaced as it drops down to Clipstone. At the Warsop Road turn right, then left at a T-junction. Follow the road through the village to your starting point. For a closer view of King John's Palace, climb the path to the Hall beside the bus shelter as you pass through the village.

12: RUFFORD & EDWINSTOWE

Though Sherwood Forest is only a shadow of its former self, with ranks of conifers replacing the greenwood, small oases remain. Two of these are Rufford Park and Edwinstowe Country Park.

Distance: 5.5 miles

Time: 2.5 hours

Start: Rufford Park car park, map reference SK 644647

Maps: Pathfinder SK 66/76 (Ollerton), Landranger 120 (Mansfield & the Dukeries)

How to get There:

By Car: Rufford Country Park is on the A614, just South of Ollerton.

By Bus: Good service from Nottingham and Ollerton.

Refreshments: Stable Block cafe, Rufford Park, Dukeries Hotel and Robin Hood, Edwinstowe

Nearest Tourist Information: Ollerton Roundabout (SK 651675), Tel 0623 824545

Rufford Abbey was founded by the Cistertian monks of Rievaulx in 1147, and though little remains of the buildings, and only fragments have survived of the series of country houses built on top of it, the grounds are now a pleasant country park owned by the County Council. Each year new improvements are made, 1990 seeing the opening of the refurbished undercroft of the monastery.

Starting in Rufford Abbey car park, walk towards the buildings. The first encountered is the stable block, where there is a shop and a series of craft exhibitions, as well as a cafe in the coach house. Turn left past the Abbey and along a tree-lined, L-shaped walk. At the end, turn left to the lake, cross the bridge on the right and follow the path round the lake. This is a sanctuary for wildlife, and a detour to the Mill, just before

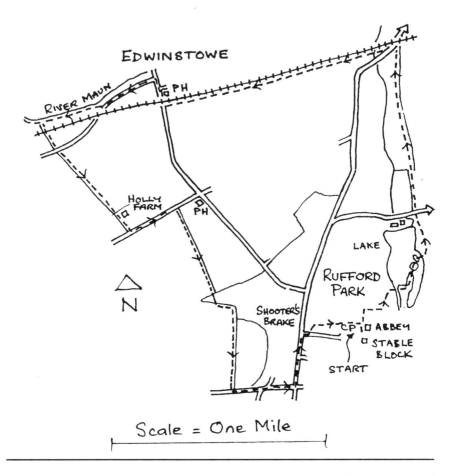

reaching the road in Rufford, will reward you with information and publications about the area and its flora and fauna.

The walk continues across the road, with mill cottages right and the ford left, then straight on along a farm track to join the A614. Cross the road carefully to a stile leading to a path alongside the railway. After crossing a footbridge, cross a stile left, then turn right to follow the edge of several fields, then a track to Edwinstowe.

At the road, turn right to go under the railway bridge and pass or visit the Dukeries Hotel. The railway now only carries mineral traffic, but the hotel was built in the 1850's to cater for the hordes of tourists who flocked by rail to Edwinstowe and its forest.

At this point, a walk through the village and past the cricket pitch would bring you to the enormously popular Sherwood Forest Visitor Centre, where there are displays and a shop offering, among other things, leaflets describing walks in the forest nearby. The detour would take about an hour, but another visit would be needed to explore this fascinating area.

After passing the Dukeries Hotel, turn left after two hundred yards along the Clipstone and Mansfield road. About fifty yards before the railway bridge, turn right along a field-edge to follow the river Maun, with its fringe of oak, alder and hawthorn. Where the river starts to swing right, turn up beside the hedge on your left to the railway, cross and continue to a road. Cross this and go straight on by the hedge, eventually passing Holly Farm and going down the drive.

Turn left along the road, then right about 100 yards before the traffic lights, unless the "Robin Hood" attracts. Walk along the track to a strip of woodland, pass through and turn left along the edge, then right down the field edge to a woodland road. Here turn left, continuing carefully ahead at the double bend in the entrance drive to "Centre Parcs" and past a 'Road Closed' sign to return past a row of rhododendrons to the A614. Cross to the pavement opposite, turn left, then right into the entrance to Rufford Abbey. To avoid cars, take a path left beside the bus turning circle. This brings you to the original drive leading to the abbey, a pleasant approach to your starting point.

Refreshments, shops, craft exhibitions and a pleasure garden await you in or behind the Stable Block.

13: WELLOW

A pleasant walk through woodland and an ancient lane, with one short climb.

Distance: 4.5 miles

Time: 2 hours

Start: Wellow village green, map reference SK 670662

Maps: Pathfinder 66/76 (Ollerton), Landranger 120 (Mansfield and the Dukeries)

How to Get There:

By Car: Wellow is on the A616 Newark to Ollerton road, just a mile or so from Ollerton

By Bus: There are regular bus services between Newark and Ollerton, but not many, and none on Sundays

Refreshments: Wellow has two pubs, the Red Lion and the Durham Ox

Nearest Tourist Information: Ollerton Roundabout (SK 651675), Tel 623 824545

Wellow is a delightful village whose Green has a fine maypole. In May each year this attracts crowds to see the traditional dancing and crowning of the May Queen. An interesting feature is the dry ditch, still partly intact, which surrounds the village and is partly followed by footpaths. Opinions differ as to whether this, like the moated site called Jordan's Castle just above the village, was prehistoric or a later creation when Wellow was in frequent dispute with the nearby Rufford Abbey.

Start at the village Green, walking away from the A616 along the Eakring road for 100 yards, and turn right at an entrance to Wellow School. The watercourse beside you is part of the mediaeval defences of the village, and you follow the tree-shaded path beside it back to the main road. Cross the road, turn left for a few yards, then head right

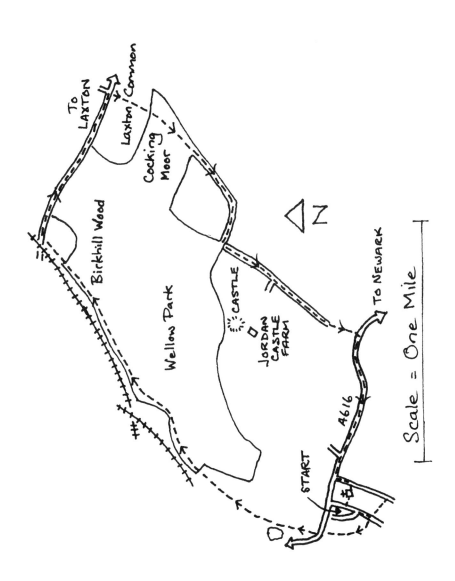

across the grass to pass to the right of the little fishing-lake, with the cricket pitch to your right.

Follow the hedged lane, keeping right at a fork, and continue along the fringe of Wellow Park Wood for about a mile. The path is bordered by a wide range of deciduous trees and wild flowers can be seen in plenty. On reaching a road, turn right towards Laxton and climb the steep hill past the Butterley brick works.

Wellow Green

At the top of the hill, continue for about 300 yards and turn right to cross Laxton Common: at this point there is a farm track opposite. A clear path leads to Cocking Moor, which despite its name consists of dense woodland. This was the Common used by the "toft-holders" (householders) of Wellow, and our route through the wood – mostly elderly hawthorn – is clearly waymarked. The next section, once a green lane for access to the common, became totally overgrown and had to have a clear path hacked through it by Nottinghamshire County Council work teams. It is now most enjoyable, as is the farm lane which continues it down the hill, a grassy track fringed by mature trees. On the right can be seen Jordan Castle Farm, the Castle itself, a prehistoric hill fortress, being just above it. A track leads off right to the farm, but the old lane continues down the hill, now reduced to a narrow track much overhung with branches, until it is clear for the last 200 yards to the A616. Turn right here to walk into Wellow village, and take the first turn left, Potter Lane. On your right is the church, and a path through the churchyard which brings you back to the Green.

14: KNEESALL & OMPTON

From any viewpoint, Kneesall stands out on its ridge, not least at night when its fine church is floodlit. The tiny hamlet of Ompton, just over the hill on the A616 to Ollerton, is part of the same parish. Much of this walk is on lanes or sandy soil and is suitable for a winter ramble.

Distance: 6.2 miles

Time: 3 hours

Start: The Angel Inn, Kneesall, map reference SK 705642

Maps: Pathfinder SK66/76 (Ollerton), Landranger 120 (Mansfield & the Dukeries)

How to Get There:

By Car: Kneesall is on the A616 Ollerton-Newark road

By Bus: There is a regular but not frequent Newark-Ollerton service. Nothing on Sundays.

Refreshments: Angel Inn, Kneesall

Nearest Tourist Information: Ollerton roundabout (SK 651675), Tel 0623 824545

When parking at the "Angel", keep to the back of the car park. Go up the hill and past the church on the main road. On your left just before the Green you will pass the Old Hall, built in the early 16th century for Sir John Hussey and recently restored, if not precisely to its original appearance, to a very high standard. Take the grassy lane on the left opposite the Green and continue to the end of this pleasant path with its colonnade of poplars. Climb a stile into a large grass field and continue down the hill. The lane resumes in the right-hand corner of the field: follow it around a bend and past the farm road to Leyfields on the right. When the lane turns left again, go straight ahead over a concrete bridge.

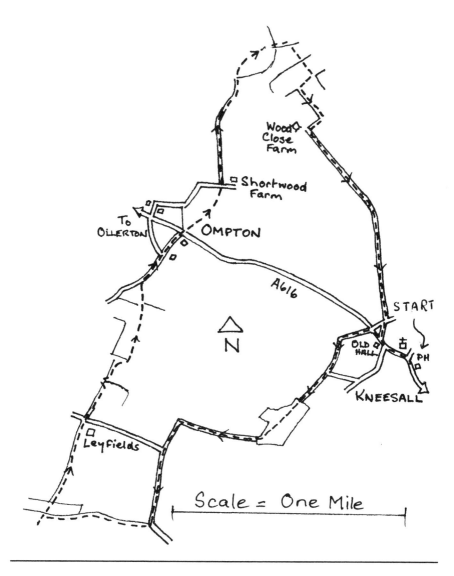

Turn right along the edge of the field, past a wood with pheasant pens, continuing to join another farm road leading to Leyfields. Turn right along the farm road, climbing the hill with Leyfields Farm among the trees to your right. Pass the farm and continue up a short hedged lane, then follow the hedge ahead. In the corner, slip left, then almost immediately right through the remains of an old lane and cross a stile. Turn left to follow the same line as before, edging right to pass a new planting of trees, and continue parallel with the left-hand hedge across two fields.

The hamlet of Ompton is now in view as you turn half-left to join a farm lane. This brings you to the A616 beside Aukland Barn. Cross the road and follow the bridleway slightly right to the gate below Shortwood Farm: if this is obstructed, follow the track ahead, then turn right.

Now follow the wide hedged lane to the end, when it continues as a track across an open field, then with a hedge on the right. Turn right through the signposted gateway, cross the field to a small gap and continue past a lone tree to the end of a hedge. Here you join a track which goes right, then swings left along a hedge and follows it right towards Wood Close Farm. Turn left along the farm track which continues as a lane into Kneesall. Turn right down the Green, then left to retrace your earlier route to the starting point and some well-earned refreshment.

Kneesall Old Hall

15: EAKRING & ROE WOOD

This walk is based on the pleasant, secluded village of Eakring, in the heart of the area once covered by Sherwood Forest. There is some outstanding deciduous woodland, including Mansey Common, former grazing land but now a truly natural "nature reserve."

Distance: 7 miles

Time: 3.5 hours

Start: Saville Arms, Eakring, map reference SK 672624

Maps: Pathfinders SK66/76 (Ollerton) and 65/75 (Newark West), Landranger 120 (Mansfield and the Dukeries)

How to Get There:

By Car: A616 from Newark, turning off at Caunton

By Bus: Occasional service from Newark and Mansfield, but not at week-ends

Refreshment: Saville Arms, Eakring

Nearest Tourist Information: Ollerton Roundabout (SK824545) Tel 0623 824545

Start at the Saville Arms, Eakring. The landlord kindly allows parking, but please go up to the car park at the top. From the pub car park, turn right, then left and right into Church Street. Go straight ahead along the unpaved lane and follow it round a double bend to the Mompesson Cross. This marks the site of the Pulpit Ash, where William Mompesson, who came from the plague village of Eyam to be rector of Eakring in 1670, had to preach due to his parishioners' fear of contagion.

Continue along the hedged lane, ignoring a green lane left, till it swings left down hill. After 200 yards take the bridleway on your right and follow it to the top of the hill. Here turn left to reach the road, then right along it to the entrance to Dukes Wood. The track leads you through

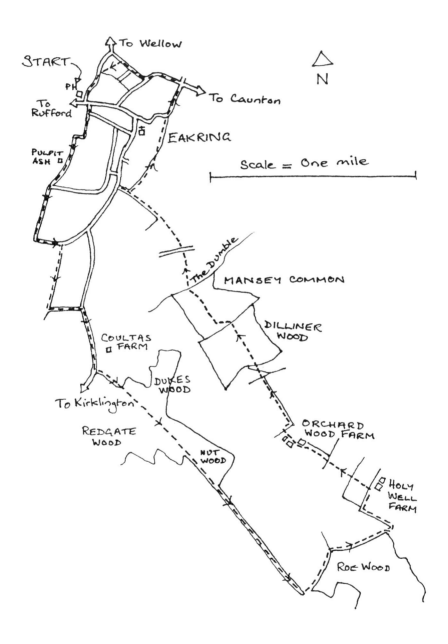

attractive woodland where "nodding donkeys" are the only sign that British Petroleum has found oil beneath Nottinghamshire's rolling farmland. At a fork, ignore the track left to a Nature Trail and keep straight ahead until you enter Whitestub Lane. Nottinghamshire County Council keep a narrow path open along this overgrown lane which contains a wealth of trees and shrubs, the most vigorous being the invasive blackthorn. Midway along, the lane is joined by the Robin Hood Way.

At the end of Whitestub Lane, cross the plank bridge left and follow the edge of Roe Wood. This ancient deciduous woodland is well stocked with wild flowers. Keep beside the wood along the edges of two fields, then cross a ditch and turn left along a track. This follows the edge of the field to Holy Well Farm, but just before the farm turn left to cross three fields to Orchard Wood Farm. You pass between the house and barns, go ahead to the next field and follow its edge right. As you descend the slope, you are heading directly for the ride through Dilliner Wood, which is reached by crossing the corners of two fields with a bridge mid-way.

Pass through the wood, which can get muddy after wet weather, to reach Mansey Common. This 40-acre common has a clear footpath across it, but otherwise is as nature intended, with hawthorn, birch and a few mighty oaks rising from a tangle of gorse and briar. There is a wealth of wildlife, relatively undisturbed as there is no easy access.

Some distance into the common, take the right-hand path and continue to cross the Dumble in its deep valley. Climb the steps to reach an open field. Your route is pretty well straight ahead: at the crest of the hill, you will see the signposts on either side of a farm road. Head for the gap in the hedge ahead, then aim for the edge of the hedge on the sky-line. Next, follow the same line with the hedge on your left to the foot of the hill. You are just short of Eakring village, but our route is right along the edges of two fields, the path edging down into woodland along the bank of a tiny stream. Join the road at the bottom of Church Hill, continue along it past three giant beeches and turn left into Sandy Lane, a hedged green lane. At a fork keep right to a point where there are stiles on both sides of the lane. Take the left-hand stile and cross the ridge-and-furrow meadow to the right-hand corner. Cross the stile and follow the road into the village to reach your starting-point and a refreshing drink.

16: KIRKLINGTON & MAYTHORNE

A country walk which really gets away from it all, but includes a delightful hamlet built round a silk mill.

Distance: 7 miles

Time: 3.5 hours

Start: Kirklington Station, map reference SK 675566

Maps: Pathfinder SK 65/75 (Newark West), Landranger 120 (Mansfield and the Dukeries)

How to Get There:

By Car: Kirklington is on the A617 Mansfield to Newark road and the station is a mile along the Edingley road

By Bus: Good service from Mansfield and Newark along the A617

Refreshments: Sorry, you'll have to carry a picnic

Nearest Tourist Information: The Ossington, Beastmarket Hill, Newark (opposite the castle) Tel 0636 78962

Starting from the car park and picnic area at Kirklington Station, walk past the station building and follow the old railway, or Southwell Trail, towards Southwell. The hawthorn and blackthorn hedges are starting to close in, but the trail is still easy to walk. On reaching a tarmac lane, turn left to pass through Maythorne, a hamlet largely built around a former silk-mill, and left across a bridge.

The mill was originally built as a cotton mill, but converted to silk and lace-thread in 1832. The mill itself has now been made into flats, with the workers' cottages around it preserved as homes. The two new houses beside the mill, though not unattractive, hardly fit in with the rest of the community.

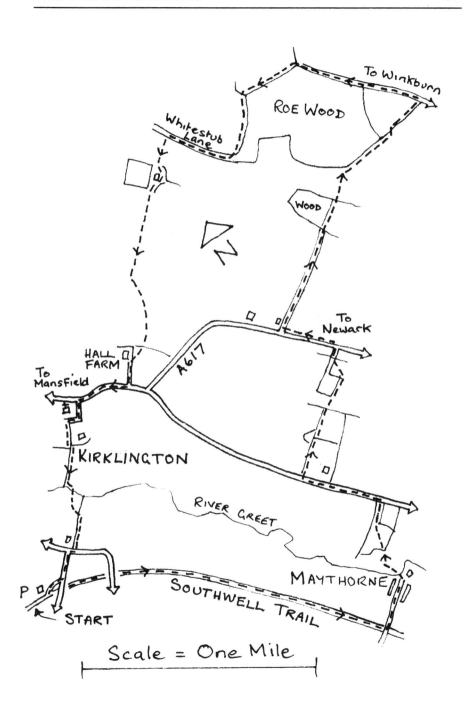

Crossing the bridge, the mill-pond on your left is home to swans and ducks who show little fear of passing walkers. Go ahead and over a stile, along the left-hand field-edge and diagonally right at the end. Cross a stile by the gate, then go left over stiles and ditchboard and on the same line as before up the hill to a gate.

Turn left for 600 yards and just past Meadow Farm look out for a stile on your right. Climb the hill, with wide views opening up over the valley and Southwell Minster peeping over the hills to the left. Continue with the hedge left, then across a field and down the side of an orchard. The path now angles left to join the drive to Brickyard Farm near the A617 road.

Turn left for about 200 yards, keeping an eye out for cars overtaking on this straight stretch of road, then right up a hedged lane. Continue along a field-edge and cross a field to Roe Wood. Turn right to walk along the edge of the wood, then beside a stream to a footbridge left. Cross this and turn right to follow the stream again to a lane. Turn left here: when the track turns away, keep on along the edge of the wood until you reach a strip of woodland known as Whitestub Lane. Cross the ditchboard and turn right along the lane.

At some waymarks, turn left along a field edge and continue along a track which drops down to Hall Farm, with glimpses of Kirklington Hall among the trees to the right. A late eighteenth century house, it is now a private school. Reaching the main road at Kirklington, turn right for 100 yards, then first left beside the church to Church Farm Cottage. Turn right as waymarked across neatly-tended grass to a kissing-gate. Turn left in the field to another kissing-gate in the corner and keep right in the next field to a footbridge. Cross this and go along the field-edge right, over a footbridge and right past Osmanthorpe Manor to a road. Turn right, then first left: now a 'Picnic Place' sign on the right brings us back to the Station.

17: FARNSFIELD CIRCLE

An easy walk around a charming Nottinghamshire village, including the well-tended woodland around the Georgian Hexgreave Hall.

Distance: 5.5 miles

Time: 2.5 hours

Start: Farnsfield church, map reference SK 646566

Maps: Pathfinder SK65/75 (Newark West), Landranger 120 (Mansfield and the Dukeries)

How to Get There:

By Car: Farnsfield is on the road between Rainworth and Southwell.

By Bus: Good service between Mansfield and Newark

Refreshments: Plough and Red Lion, Farnsfield

Nearest Tourist Office: The Ossington, Beastmarket Hill, Newark (opposite the castle) Tel 0636 78962

From Farnsfield's lofty Victorian church, angle right across the road to go up New Hill, which becomes Broomfield Lane and crosses the Southwell Trail. This is a disused railway line which the County Council have adopted as a Trail for walkers: it could be used to shorten the walk.

Continue past South Lodge, with its imposing gate-posts, along a quiet lane leading only to a couple of farms. At a T-junction, turn right and cross the stile left just round the corner. Cross the field diagonally: if this footpath is obstructed by crops as usual, continue along the road, turn left along the tree-lined lane for half a mile.

The cross-field path joins this estate road lined with majestic lime trees. After passing Hexgreave Hall hidden among its trees, we must find a right turn through the woodland. After passing a short forest track on the right, ending at a white gate with ornate pillars, turn through the

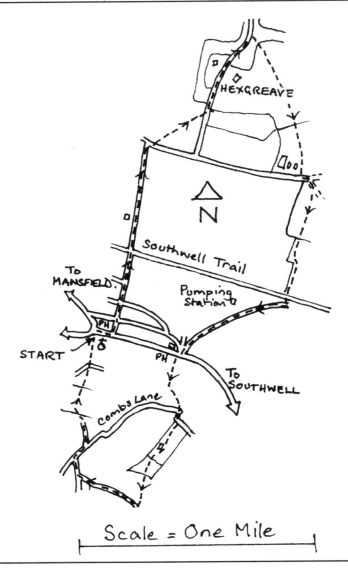

trees after the 8th lime tree on the right. At a stile, go diagonally across the field, passing first a chestnut tree, then an oak, to a gate left of the farm buildings. As you cross this ploughed parkland, the late eighteenth century Hall can be seen on your right.

Turn left for a few yards, then choose the right-hand of two farm tracks. Turn right along another track to a gap, then follow the right-hand side of the field to the Southwell Trail. Cross the track and take one of the little paths into Brickyard Lane, then follow it to Farnsfield Main Street. The Plough Inn is on your right, our route is down a walled ginnel almost opposite. Cross the stile at the end and turn left along the meadow to a stile and Cotton Mill Lane.

Turn left and follow the lane for a few yards round the corner, then go ahead past the sports pavilion to a hand-gate. Follow the path across a grass field to a stile, then continue to a hedged path. Turn right along it, then turn right at a farm-road leading to Riddings Hill Farm. Go right again along a metalled road as far as a bridleway left. Follow it to cross a stile and continue to a handgate: go straight across two paddocks to a metalled road, then along the ginnel opposite. Now keep right to return to your starting point.

18: HALAM & OXTON

Robin Hood's fame in Nottinghamshire has led to all manner of obscure caves, grottoes and wells being named after him. Just north of the attractive village of Oxton is Robin Hood Hill, the site of an ancient burial mound. In the pasture below is the best-preserved pre-Roman fort in the county, known as Oldox.

Distance: 10 miles

Time: 5 hours

Start: Near Halam Pumping Station, map reference SK 667536

Maps: Pathfinder 65/75 (Newark West) and 64/74 (Carlton & Elston), Landranger 120 (Mansfield and the Dukeries) and 129 (Nottingham and Loughborough)

How to Get There:

By Car: Halam is on the minor road between Southwell and Farnsfield.

By Bus: There is a reasonable service between Mansfield and Southwell.

Refreshments: Green Dragon, Oxton

Nearest Tourist Office: The Ossington, Beastmarket Hill, Newark (opposite the castle) Tel 0636 78962

Opposite the Pumping Station is Cutlersforth Lane, a pleasant hedged lane which you follow up the hill. After a quarter of a mile ignore the right-hand bend and follow the green lane ahead, now traffic-free and a linear nature reserve. As well as the flora and fauna, you can enjoy glimpses of extensive views on both sides of this ridge road when the hedges permit. At the end turn right away from Turncroft Farm, with views to Farnsfield and beyond opening up ahead of you, and at the next bend turn left down an ancient holloway. A stick could be helpful here, as nettles tend to take over, but it is soon possible to climb the

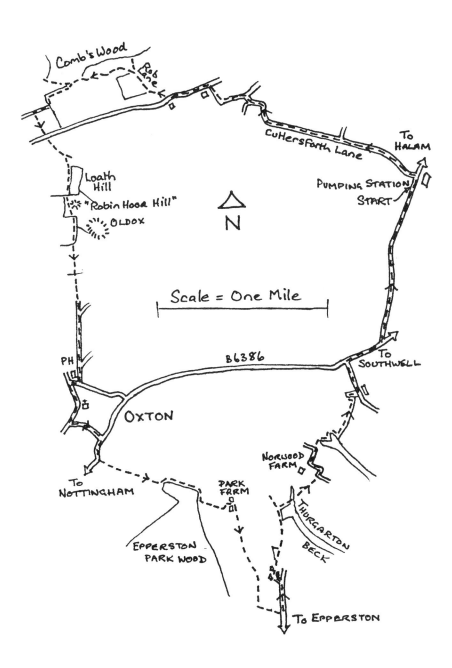

bank right and continue along the field edge. The path swings down hill to pass right of the farm buildings to Greaves Lane.

Turn left along the lane for 250 yards, then opposite some cottages turn right into Rob Lane. It seems unlikely that this narrow steep-sided valley ever saw wheeled traffic, but pack-horses or ramblers should have no trouble. At the top of this sharp climb, turn left at a signpost. After about half a mile another sign guides you left into a field. Turn right along the top of the field and round the corner to a gateway, with fine views West over rolling countryside. The main feature to be seen is the woodland, reminiscent of Sherwood Forest which once covered this county from Nottingham to Worksop. Sadly much that remains is regimented conifers.

Go through the gateway and along the farm track to an oak tree. Turn left as signposted and cross the field to Greaves Lane. Cross the road and follow the farm track until opposite the corner of Loath Hill wood on the right. Walk to the right of the wood, pass through a handgate at the end, then pass to the right of Robin Hood Hill and between it and the tumulus beyond. This is a fine place to stop for a picnic and enjoy the view, but also a very ancient site. The conical tumulus, obviously a burial site has not, as far as I know, been excavated. The ancient fort in the grassland to the south-east is a complex system of defensive ramparts and ditches which was here before the Romans came.

Keep along the meadowside to a stile, along 100 yards of farm track till it turns away, then cross a stile and continue on the same line across two fields to Windmill Hill Lane. A stroll up from Oxton to Robin Hood's Hill being popular, this path gets well trodden. The lane leads you to Oxton by the Green Dragon, where good food and drinks are available. Turn right and immediately left, passing Oxton church which would reward a visit. Turn left again along New Road, which becomes Sandy Lane after the ford and footbridge. At the end turn right, then after 100 yards left into the entrance to Park Farm.

Continue to the farm, through the yard and along the farm track for over a mile. Plantings of a variety of trees, mainly oak, ash and field maple enhance this part of the route. Where it joins a metalled road go left up the hill and left again at Cottage Farm. Keep right past Keeper's Cottage. After half a mile, at the crown of the hill, pass a wood and turn right along its edge and cross a wooded gully, the top end of Thurgarton Beck. Continue to a farm lane which you follow ahead, swinging left, then right but keeping straight on at the next bend. Follow the right-hand hedge in a circuitous route, rounding a tongue of woodland and following the edge of a large field, finally passing through a gate right to pass through a small wood to a farm road.

Turn left to reach a road, turn right along the road to the first left signposted 'Halam'. This brings you after three quarters of a mile to your starting point.

19: LOWDHAM & EPPERSTONE

This short walk links two lovely churches and two mills, all in beautiful settings. A gradual climb up an ancient lane brings you to a ridge providing extensive views on both sides.

Distance: 5 miles

Time: 2.5 hours

Start: Lowdham church, map reference SK 664467

Maps: Pathfinder SK 64/74 (Carlton & Elston) and Landranger 129 (Nottingham & Loughborough)

How to get There:

By Car: Lowdham lies on both sides of the A6097 near its junction with the A612

By Bus: Lowdham is well served from Nottingham and Southwell

By Train: Lowdham station is on the Nottingham to Lincoln line. It is a mile from the church.

Refreshments: Cross Keys, Epperstone

Nearest Tourist Information: Wheeler Gate, Nottingham Tel 0602 470661

Start at Lowdham church, keeping clear of any gates. The church, in its wooded setting, is set back from the road, and is now separated from most of its village by the A6097. Walk up the lane beside the church and turn right after a hundred yards. The path follows a field edge, passes through a tiny spinney, and joins an accommodation road to reach the A6097. Cross this with great care and angle left to enter the drive to Lowdham Mill.

The earliest records of the mill are from 1662, but there was certainly a mill on the site much earlier. It was working until 1946, when Mr Walter

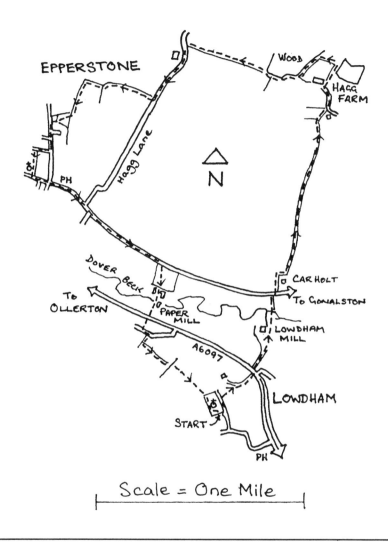

Scale = One Mile

Carby retired from the job he had started as an apprentice 53 years before.

In its idyllic setting on the Dover Beck, the mill, with its tree-fringed mill pond and neatly-tended garden gives more pleasure to the passing walker than do many larger and statelier homes.

As the drive swings slightly left, go through the bridlegate ahead, through an orchard and across the bridge, with a view through weeping willows of the Mill House. Pass the side of the mill buildings and continue beside the mill stream with its row of pollarded willows to a gate. A fenced path brings you to the road. Turn right for a few yards, then left past Car Holt Farm. Take the signposted route along the field-edge to the left of the farm, veer a little right at the end then up the hill between hedges. This narrow lane is clearly a very ancient route, and may have been part of a direct route from Nottingham to Southwell.

At the top of the lane continue by the side of a high, dense hedgerow, over a bridge, and bear right past a majestic oak to a farm-track. Turn left, follow the track and pass right of Gonalston Hagg Farm and down the hill. Blue bridleway signs indicate a left turn below the farm, where a screen of trees is newly planted. On reaching the wood, turn left again to climb the hill, then right to continue alongside the wood. A circuitous route, but the more obvious track above Hagg Farm is not registered as a right of way. At the end of the wood veer right then left again to follow the hedge to a road.

Turn left here, pass Eastwood Farm and after 200 yards cross a stile on the right. Epperstone church is now in view, nestling in the trees below. Follow the field edge, cross the stile where a tree stump seems to have fossilised fungus. Go along the top of the next field to the corner, then left down the hill. On reaching a footbridge on the right, cross it into a ridge and furrow paddock. Angle slightly left to a stile which is only seen at the last minute. Continue along a very narrow path to a set of steps and Chapel Lane, Epperstone.

Follow the lane left and turn right into Church Lane. Notice a dovecote on your right as you walk up to the churchyard. Pass through the kissing-gate into this idyllic place, walking beside a row of gigantic beech, larch and chestnut to the church, which deserves a visit. Go down the steps to main Street and turn left past the shop and 'Cross Keys'. Notice the tiny dovecote opposite. Go straight on along Gonalston Road, which you follow for about half a mile. Clearly an old drove road, it has wide grass verges for walkers and horse riders. Go through a white gate on the right and through the Mill. The neat white Old Mill House, stables and fencing make a beautiful picture. Pass the paper-mill itself and join the A6097.

Cross it and carry on along a narrow path between hedge and fence to the old road. Turn left, then shortly right up a track, turning left after a hedge. Follow this to a stile then straight on, heading to the right of Lowdham church and your starting point.

Lowdham Mill

20: HOVERINGHAM & CAYTHORPE

A short walk follows a fine stretch of the river Trent and explores its tributary, the Dover Beck, to find two water-mills

Distance: 5 miles

Time: 2.5 hours

Start: Reindeer Inn, Hoveringham, map reference SK 699468

Maps: Pathfinder SK64/74 (Carlton & Elston), Landranger 129 (Nottingham & Loughborough)

How to Get There:

By Car: From the A612 Nottingham/Southwell road, turning off at Gonalston or Thurgarton.

By Bus: Good service from Nottingham and Newark

Refreshments: Reindeer and Marquis of Granby, Hoveringham, Black Horse, Caythorpe

Nearest Tourist Information: Wheeler Gate, Nottingham, Tel 0602 470661

The Dover Beck runs into the river Trent near Caythorpe. Along its length can be found a string of water-mills, once the centre of village life, but now private residences. The walk takes in two mills mentioned in the rent rolls of 1328 for the adjoining parish of Thurgarton, mills then known as "Barailium" and "Snelling" but now more simply as Hoveringham and Caythorpe mills.

Start at the Reindeer in Hoveringham. Walk down a track left of the Reindeer into a sports field, around the right-hand side and down the edge of two fields to join a bridleway, crossing two ditchboards en route. Turn left to reach a road, cross and follow the waymarked route ahead. Go through a gate left at the end of the field, then turn right to pass Hoveringham Mill. The mill was worked until 1961, and shows its origins clearly. In fact the machinery is still intact, but is not normally open to view. The present building was erected in 1779 and the adjoining house extended in 1845.

Cross the bridge over the Dover Beck, to reach a gate and turn left immediately. Cross a stile and follow the hedge for 150 yards, then turn left again to follow the Dover Beck to Caythorpe. Turn left to pass through the village; the Mill is almost opposite the pub. Continue for 250 yards beyond the village and cross a stile right. Follow the field edge and keep left between hedges at the end to reach the Trentside meadows. Go on to the river bank and turn left along it, passing through a gate midway, to join the road again just short of the old Elm Tree inn, now being converted to homes.

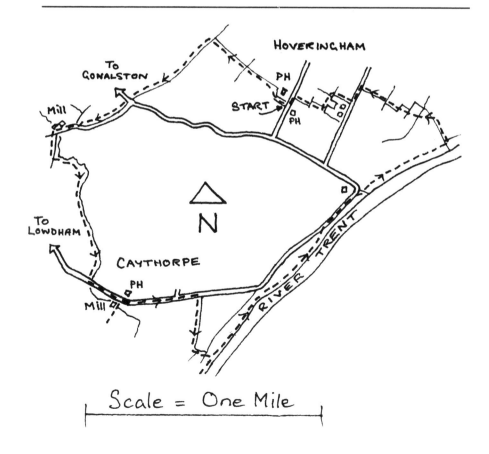

On the corner rejoin the river bank, pass through the gate and follow the Trent to the next gate. Pass through and turn left immediately to follow an overgrown path just inside land bordering the old gravel pit, now used for sailing. Cross a stile left and cut off the corner of the meadow to another stile. Cross an open field, continue with the hedge right. After another stile go ahead with a newly-planted spinney, then a hedge left to reach a hedged lane. Turn left, cross the stile just before the houses, and go on to a tiny spinney. Pass through it, cross the stile and go ahead to the next one. Now turn right along the hedge to a footbridge, which leads via a small birch wood and a narrow ginnel to the main street. Turn left to return to your starting point.

To extend the walk by three miles from Caythorpe, turn right in Caythorpe along the front of the Mill, follow the waymarked path to Gunthorpe, turn left to reach the river, then follow the towpath back to Hoveringham.

21: HALLOUGHTON & THURGARTON

At Thurgarton the road east from Nottingham leaves the Trent valley and roller-coasters its way to the 'cathedral village' of Southwell. This is splendid walking and riding country, and most of this walk is on bridleways, sometimes crossing the deeply-cut streams known hereabouts as Dumbles

Distance: 8.5 miles

Time: 4 hours

Start: Halloughton, map reference SK691517

Maps: Pathfinders SK65/75 (Newark West) and 64/74 (Carlton & Elston), Landrangers 120 (Mansfield & the Dukeries) and 129 (Nottingham & Loughborough)

How to Get There:

By Car: Halloughton is just off the A612 Nottingham to Newark road, a mile or so west of Southwell.

By Bus: There are regular services passing the end of the village

Refreshments: Coach & Horses and Red Lion, Thurgarton

Nearest Tourist Information: Wheeler gate, Nottingham, Tel 0602 470661

On arriving at Halloughton, would drivers pass the church and park beside the brick barn just beyond Manor Farm House. This avoids obstruction of this narrow lane. The barn doors are never opened.

Return to the main road and walk 200 yards towards Nottingham, passing through the signposted gate on your left. Walk along the field edge to Gypsy Lane, with perhaps a glimpse of Brackenhurst Hall on the hill-top left. This became an agricultural college in 1949. You will soon find red or green waymarks which show Farm Trails around the estate, and information boards provide an interesting commentary on the work done.

On reaching Gypsy Lane, turn left for 150 yards, then right just before a gate, as signposted. Go along the track to a gap, where you turn left and follow the top edge of a long field. At the end, turn right down a track marked by newly-planted ash trees towards the Dumble. Crossing the bridge, go round the left-hand side of the next field and along the top as far as a farm road leading down to the railway. The Trent valley opens up here, with wooded hills rising steeply across the river.

Turn right just over the level crossing and follow the field edge round a spinney to the next field. Keep along the left-hand side of this narrow field, switching to the other side of the hedge to join a track: this brings

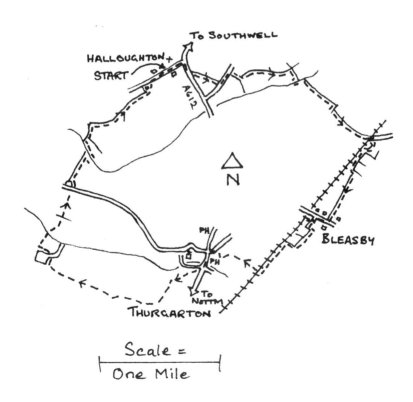

you into Bleasby. Turn right along the street, then left along the lane to Bleasby Church of England school. Go straight ahead through a hand gate and along a track which follows the edge of two fields. On reaching a short section of hedged path, turn right to the railway, then left to follow it until you reach a farm track and a level crossing. Beyond this point there is ample evidence of sand and gravel extraction, an industry which is gradually chewing its way across the plain, leaving fishing- and boating-lakes behind it.

Turn right to cross the line and follow the track, bearing left where it forks. In the grass field behind the farm bear right and along a ginnel to the road. Turn left, left again at the A612 and pass the Coach and Horses. Just beyond on the left is a splendid clock, salvaged from Nottingham station and erected here by Mr. Hoggard of Priory Farm. In niches on nearby walls are the heads of Queen Elizabeth the First and Mithras, the god of light.

Cross the road to the Priory gates. Go straight ahead past the Lodge along a fenced path, angle left to the fence and follow it to a handgate. Turn left and follow the fence, turning right at the top. In the valley can be seen Thurgarton church, all that remains of a Benedictine Priory, and beside it an eighteenth century house, now the property of Boots the Chemists.

The bridleway you are now following keeps to the ridge along the top of several fields, then drops down to a narrow strip of woodland. Pass through and keep left, then right around the field to a bridge over Thurgarton Dumble beside an old sheep-dip.

Go slightly right up the hill and along a track to the farm road. Turn right for fifteen yards, then left through a gate and around the left-hand edge of the field. A footbridge crosses Halloughton Dumble, the bridleway turns left beside the dumble to the end of the field, then right to continue beside the field boundary. On reaching a farm road, turn right, still beside the hedgerows, pass through a tiny spinney and go on until you reach a track. This leads through a farm yard and into the village street of Halloughton beside Bridle Way Farm.

Turn right to your starting point, taking the opportunity to admire Manor Farm House. Once a prebendal house of Southwell, it has a mediaeval tower, an extension of about 1600 whose half-timbered construction is hard to distinguish, and finally a Georgian wing. Five centuries of domestic architecture in a sylvan setting.

Manor Farm, Halloughton

22: KIRKLINGTON, WESTHORPE EDINGLEY

A highly recommended walk between peaceful and attractive villages, with a Stately Home and fine panoramas.

Distance: 7.25 miles

Time: 3.5 hours

Start: Kirklington Station, map reference SK 675566

Maps: Pathfinder SK 65/75 (Newark West), Landranger 120 (Mansfield and the Dukeries)

How to Get There:

By Car: Kirklington is on the A617 Mansfield to Newark road. Its station is on the Edingley road.

By Bus: Good services between Mansfield and Newark

By Train: Sorry, they took the lines up in 1956

Refreshments: Lord Nelson, Westhorpe, Old Reindeer, Edingley

Nearest Tourist Information: The Ossington, Beastmarket Hill, Newark (opposite the castle) Tel 0636 78962

Start at the grassy car park beside Kirklington Station on the Southwell Trail. This linear park was created by Nottinghamshire County Council from the old Midland Railway line, last used in 1956. Pass the station house and follow the trail right for about a mile and a half. Trees line the route, mostly ash, and a variety of small shrubs, mainly hawthorn and blackthorn, have taken over to reduce the trail to a narrow path. However, it is easily walkable and a haven for wild life.

The next paved road leads left to Maythorne, a hamlet based on the old mill which produced cotton and then silk there. However our route is

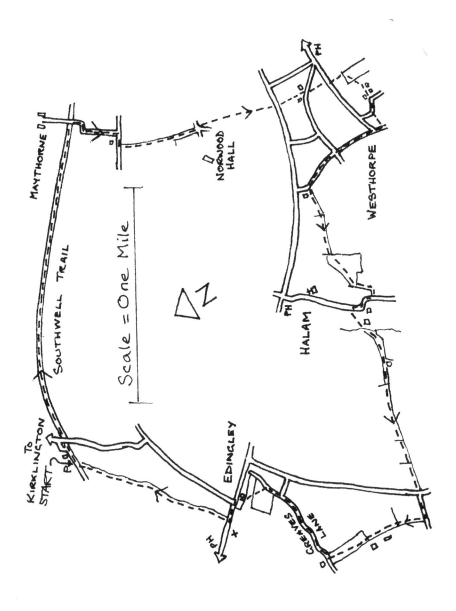

right to the main road, right again for 100 yards, then left to pass through the grounds of Norwood House. Just after passing a cross-road the house itself can be seen on the right, an impressive 5-bay brick house built in 1764. The route at this point is ahead along a grassy track between ranks of apple trees, then beside small arable fields, formerly orchards before the apple glut of 1989. Cross the Halam Road, a tiny flagstone bridge and the field beyond, heading just to the right of a brick house.

Go straight ahead across the B6386, unless you need refreshment which can be had at the Admiral Nelson to your left. Continue down a ginnel between garden hedges and walls to Westhorpe. Cross the road half-right to another ginnel leading to a small paddock which has the distinctive ridges of ancient ploughland. Cross the bridge and angle right to a kissing-gate. Pass through a group of pleasant houses to a road: turn right, go round the corner and cross the field left.

Turn right to rejoin the road, then go up the hill to cross the B6386. Follow Saversick Lane past some ancient willows, then turn left into the drive of "Halam Gate", following the fence through the garden, then past neat rows of Bramleys and other apple trees. Cross a stile and drop down to Halam, heading leftish to a stile in the corner of the pasture. An old lane brings you to the road, which you follow right, around a double bend. At this point, there are two pubs ahead in the centre of Halam.

Take the footpath left along the farm road behind Manor Farm and past the tennis courts to a footbridge. Cross two stiles and turn right up the hill past Machin's Farm, whose renovation has included extensive tree-planting beside the footpath. Continue along field-edges, with wide views opening up on all sides, and a multi-coloured crop of rose bushes beside part of the path. Cross Newhall Lane and continue up Turncroft Lane opposite. Cross a stile right and follow the edge of two fields, passing New Hall Farm. This is the highest point of the walk, with wide views and very little sign of habitation below you. This changes as you drop down through the remains of an orchard to reach Greaves Lane, opposite Allesford House, with Elkesley to your right and Farnsfield left.

Turn right along Greaves Lane, ignoring a right turn to Mansfield and Newark, then turning left through the next field-gate. Cross two fields and pass through the well-tended garden of a cottage to Edingley Main

Street and turn left. Our route is over the stile on the right, but if refreshments are needed the "Old Reindeer" is a hundred yards beyond, just past the tiny church guarded by an enormous sycamore.

The walk continues beside the tiny Edingley Beck to rejoin the Southwell Trail.

23: SOUTHWELL ROUND

Whichever way you approach Southwell, the twin towers of its Minster dominate the skyline. Though the town is attractive, our walk skirts the fringes to visit a fruit-farm, two mills and traces of the Midland railway.

Distance: 5 miles

Time: 2.5 hours

Maps: Pathfinder SK 65/75 (Newark West), Landranger 120 (Mansfield & the Dukeries).

Start: Church Street car park, map reference SK 702539

How to Get There:

By Car: A617 and 612 from Newark, B6386 from Nottingham

By Bus: Good services from Nottingham and Newark

Refreshments: Admiral Nelson, Newcastle Arms and many others in Southwell

Nearest Tourist Information: Ossington, Beastmarket Hill, Newark (opposite the castle) Tel 0636 78962

Starting in the car-park off Church Street, cross the road and pass the west front of the Minster. This lovely church, the cathedral of Nottinghamshire since 1884, was built in the twelfth century and thankfully has been little 'improved', though the 13th century Chapter House is perhaps its most beautiful feature. It is worth getting to know better, and guidance is offered in the transept bookshop. Pass the Bishop's Manor to reach the graceful arches of the war memorial. Pass through and follow the avenue of lime trees beside the sports field, then turn left down to the Potwell Dyke and along a path, swinging right to reach the Nottingham Road. Walk away from the town about 300 yards to a bridleway on the right. This begins as an overgrown lane, then goes along the edge of two fields. In the second, go right through a gateway.

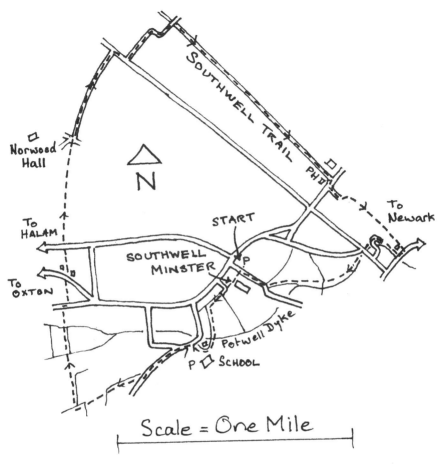

The well-trodden path follows a hedge and then descends an open field with a fine view of the tree-lined Dumble and beyond it, Westhorpe. This was an independent village, and though absorbed by Southwell keeps its own character. Climb down to the bridge over the Dumble, then cross a small grass field to another footbridge. Walk up a hedged ginnel to the street, then cross half-right to another ginnel leading to the Oxton road. For those in need of refreshment, the Admiral Nelson is to the right, but our route is across the road and straight across an arable field to a stile, heading for the gap beside the stag-headed oak beyond Halam Road.

After crossing the road you enter the orchards of Norwood Hall, whose owner Sir John Starkey has developed his estate as a thriving fruit farm. Southwell is the home of the Bramley apple, which is still grown here. Pass between fruit trees and arable land, then regimented ranks of apples, with a view of Norwood Hall to the left. The house was built in 1764. After the orchards carry straight on to the Kirklington road, turn right, then left after 100 yards. This road takes you to the Southwell Trail, a linear park created by Nottinghamshire County Council from the old Midland railway line. This section of the line, from Southwell to Mansfield, was opened in 1871 to carry coal, milk, passengers and later oil from the Eakring field.

Norwood Hall, Southwell

Turn right to follow the Trail to the end: to your left is Cauldwell's Mill, at least the third to occupy the site, rebuilt in 1893 after a fire. It is now converted to flats. The Newcastle Arms, a few yards to the right, was built to serve Southwell station. Cross the road to enter Riverside, and angle left to join the Greet. Follow the pleasantly-landscaped path through the site of the railway station to Newark road, turn right in front of the railway cottage and right again. This is the Potwell Dyke again: follow this into a cul-de-sac, turn left and go ahead when the road swings away. Cross a street to the footpath at the corner of Burgage Lane and follow this along grass fields beside the Dyke, to a tarmac path. After crossing this the Minster comes in sight, and you have only to cross one meadow to Church Street and turn right to return to the car park.

24: SOUTHWELL & MORTON

The rolling countryside between Southwell and the Trent valley is criss-crossed by a series of paths, linking the smaller villages with their "metropolis". Two of these make a popular local walk.

Distance: 7 miles

Time: 3.5 hours

Start: Hearty Good Fellow, Easthorpe, map reference SK 706537

Maps: Pathfinder 65/75 (Newark West), Landranger 120 (Mansfield & the Dukeries)

How to Get There:

By Car: The start is in Easthorpe, Southwell, reached via the A612 from Newark or the B6386 from Nottingham

By Bus: There is a frequent service from Newark, Nottingham or Mansfield

Refreshments: Hearty Good Fellow, Southwell, Full Moon, Morton

Nearest Tourist Information: The Ossington, Beastmarket Hill, Newark, Tel 0636 78962

Start at the Hearty Good Fellow, parking in Easthorpe or in nearby streets, and walk down Shady Lane on the right hand side. Cross a footbridge and after 20 yards climb the bank left and go along the field-edge. Cross a stile to reach Church Street: cross it and continue to an archway into the Minster grounds.

This glorious Norman cathedral was built in the twelfth century and apart from some expansion and the addition of the incomparable chapter house a century later, has been little "improved". Guide books are on sale in the transept bookshop.

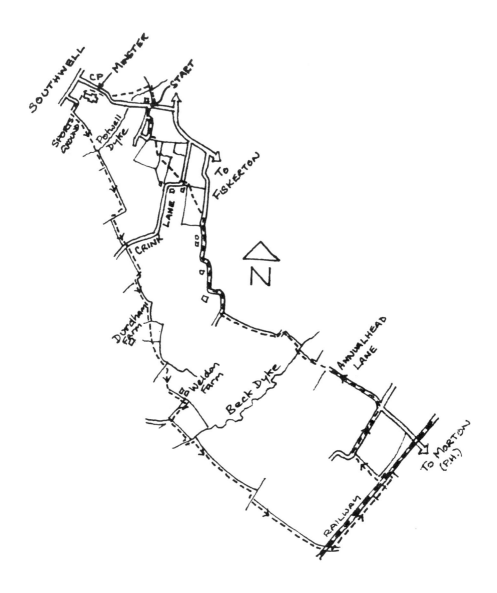

Go round the Minster to the opposite corner, pass through a narrow gateway, along a footpath and a short street to the Memorial gate.

Southwell Minster

Turn left past the bowling green and tennis courts and cross the footbridge ahead. Go up the hill with a fence right, then a hedge left. Cross a stile and at the top, go 40 yards right to a stile. Go up the hill to Crink Lane, cross it and continue along the track ahead. This swings right through a gap, then left along the sinuous edge of a large field.

Go through the left-hand gate and follow the hedge to a hand-gate. Head along the left hand fence to the corner of the meadow, cross the stile and angle across the next field to pass right of Weldon Farm buildings.

Go ahead through a gap in the hedge and a strip of woodland, then right along the field-edge. In the next field you will find a notice board erected by Brackenhurst College as part of its farm trail. Turn left here along the remains of a hedged lane to the corner and along the bottom to a footbridge.

Pass through the handgate and keep around the left-hand edge of the field to a gate in the top hedge. This leads to a lane which you follow down the hill, with a panoramic view over the Trent valley, and across the railway. Turn left over a stile just past the crossing and follow the fence along a large field and two small meadows to a gate left. Cross the track and a bridge and turn left to reach a field, where you turn right to reach Middlefield Road, an old lane.

Turn right to reach a road, then immediately left into Annualhead Lane. If you need refreshments, a right turn here brings you directly to the Full Moon in Morton. Do not turn left at the top of the field, but go straight on, cross a wide bridge and turn right then left along a field edge. Go through the gap at the end, left along a fenced section, over a bridge and then right to reach Pollard's Lane.

Turn right and walk about half a mile. Pass 2 pairs of semi-detached houses, then soon cross a stile left. Cross the field diagonally and in the corner, cross into the allotment. Turn left to Crink Lane and cross it to a stile. The path now heads across pasture land to a stile half-way down the edge of the wood; passing through the wood to another stile, continue along the same line, cross-field to a stile. Cross the stile, go along the field-edge left to another stile and along a narrow ginnel to Farthingate Close. Turn right, then right again to return to Easthorpe, and perhaps to the hospitality of the Hearty Good Fellow.

25: ROLLESTON

An easy Trent Valley walk through three beautiful villages, with riverside paths and pub.

Distance: 4.7 miles

Time: 2 hours

Start: Rolleston church, map reference SK 742526

Maps: Pathfinder SK65/75 (Newark West), Landranger 120 (Mansfield and the Dukeries)

How to Get There:

By Car: By the A612, leaving it at Thurgarton if coming from Nottingham and by the A617, turning off at Averham, if coming from Newark

By Bus: Rolleston is quite well served by Mansfield-Newark buses, though Sunday is patchy

By Train: The Nottingham to Lincoln line has a station at Rolleston and there is a regular service

Refreshments: Full Moon, Morton, Bromley Arms, Fiskerton, The Crown Inn, Rolleston

Nearest Tourist Information: The Ossington, Beastmarket Hill, Newark (opposite the Castle) Tel 0636 78962

Start the walk at Rolleston church: a typical Notts church, it is basically Norman with thirteenth century improvements. Its arcades are much admired by church architecture buffs. Take the main path through the churchyard to the left-hand corner and go straight down the field beyond to a plank bridge and stile. Go ahead and alongside the river Greet to a footbridge, then keep right of the hedge to another bridge. Continue to follow the hedge to a road. Turn left into Fiskerton and after 150 yards, just beyond the Stable salon, turn right along a narrow path. This brings you to a cul-de-sac: cross to the far side and take the tarmac

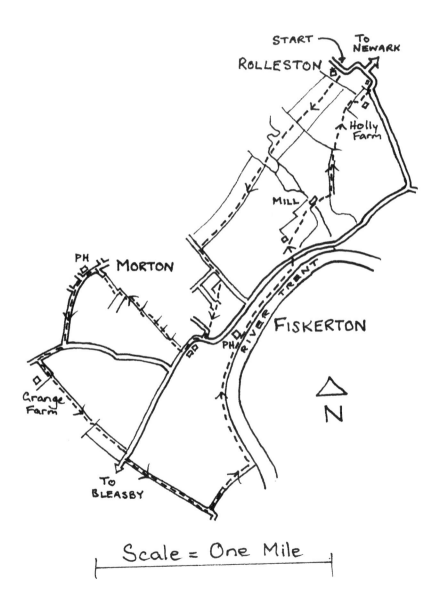

Scale = One Mile

path left. There is a choice of paths here, the one ahead leading to the Bromley arms and a short cut if only a short stroll is wanted. Our route is to the right, then straight ahead to Gravelly Lane. Continue past the Methodist Chapel and turn right along the road.

Just around the corner cross a stile on the right opposite The Homestead. The path to Morton, though almost straight, tends to hop from one side of the fence to the other, but is clearly waymarked. As you approach the village there is a path to the left, but our route is ahead across a footbridge, a few yards left then right again between two gardens. On reaching the village street, turn left to pass the Full Moon – if strictly necessary – and continue through the village, ignoring a road on your left. Turn left into the drive to Fiskerton Grange Farm and keep ahead along a field edge. At the end, cross a stile slightly left, then continue across the meadow to the road.

Turn right for a few yards, then left along a hedged lane almost to the end. Here, another green lane goes left: crossing the stile at the end, continue to the Trent floodbank. Turn left along this popular stretch of riverside, keeping an eye out for herons, and pass the Bromley Arms – again if strictly necessary – and several attractive early nineteenth century houses. At the end of the village, go up to the road and cross to approach the isolated house ahead. The path leads from beside this house to the Mill which is to the right, across an arable field. Unfortunately the adjacent floodbank is not a legal right of way.

Go through the farm gates to reach the Mill, an imposing four-storey building straddling the river Greet, pass in front of it and cross a stile. The path continues along the edge of a field to a footbridge. Turn left along the tree-lined floodbank, cross a stile and continue along the bank. After another stile, the path is being diverted slightly left to pass the yard of Holly Farm, where new housing is planned. The route will be well waymarked. The path turns right towards the farm, then left to the main road in Rolleston. Turn left around a double bend, then on past the Manor to return to the church.

26: UPTON & MORTON

A walk on the fringe of the Trent valley, passing two mills, two churchyards and a pub

Distance: 6.5 miles

Time: 3 hours

Start: "French Horn", Upton, map reference SK 738544

Maps: Pathfinder SK 65/75 (Newark West), Landranger 120 (Mansfield and the Dukeries)

How to Get There:

By Car: Upton is on the A612 between Newark and Southwell

By Bus: Sketchy service between Mansfield and Newark

Refreshments: French Horn, Upton, Full Moon, Morton

Nearest Tourist Information: Ossington, Beastmarket Hill, Newark (opposite the castle) Tel 0636 78962

A linear village astride the busy road from Newark to Southwell and thence to Nottingham, Upton has a high proportion of attractive buildings, mostly red-brick and pantiled. The glaring exception is the Hall, a Grecian-style creation complete with portico and dome, built in 1830 and now housing the Royal Horological Society.

Start at the "French Horn", Upton, parking in the grassy overflow car park at the back. From here, turn left along the path to Carr Lane. Follow this lane to the right down hill and continue till you cross a bridge over Car Dyke. When the lane ends, continue beside a hedge, then diagonally left across the field to reach an overflow from the River Greet. Cross the farm bridge and walk along the river bank towards Rolleston, with the Greet on your right and Southwell race course beyond.

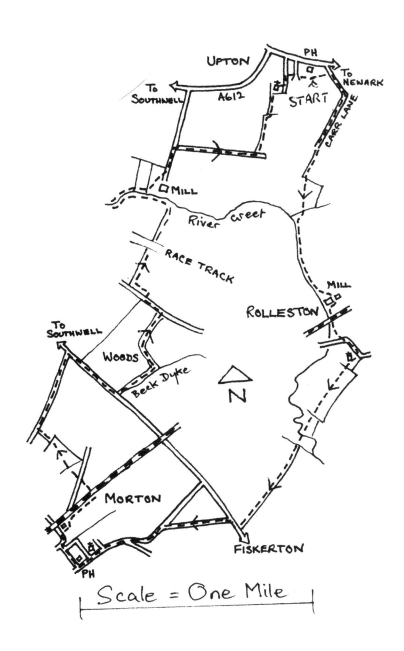

Scale = One Mile

At Rolleston Mill, cross the stile into the yard, turn right past the buildings and cross the railway with care. Cross the race course car park towards Rolleston church, enter the gate and pass through the churchyard. There should be a gap into the field behind and a clear path to the waymarked earth bridge and stile at the other end. Go on past a meander in the Greet to a new bridge, on to another bridge and the straight path to Fiskerton. Turn right, then left into Claypit Lane. At the end turn left into Morton. At the "Full Moon", where refreshments are available, turn right and go almost to the railway crossing.

Take the signposted path right and follow the left-hand edge for about a quarter mile. Cross the railway line left, then cross an old railway track into a field with a stile in the left-hand corner. After crossing, go half-right towards a gateway then straight ahead to a lane. Turn right to reach the Southwell Road, turn right, cross the old railway bridge and take the footpath left. Go down some steep steps and follow the Car Dyke bank till you reach a footbridge.

Do not cross the bridge, turn left, then shortly right beside a very high fence to join the old Southwell-Fiskerton railway. Turn left, then right into a field. Walk round the left-hand edge, cross a bridge and the race-track and continue right of the hedge to the Greet beside Upton Mill. Turn left and follow the river as far as a footbridge, then cross and return on the other bank. In the last field before the Mill go half-left towards a bridge. Turn away from the Mill and enter Green Meadow Lane, which you follow for half a mile. Take a stile left and walk up the hill towards the nine pinnacles of Upton church. After passing through the graveyard, turn right past the church and left along Church Lane. A ginnel on the right takes you into a cul-de-sac: slip right to another ginnel on your left which brings you back to the "French Horn".

27: UPTON & MICKLEBARROW HILL

From the pleasant village of Upton, a narrow ribbon of houses along the A612, this walk uses mainly green lanes and meadowland paths with surprisingly few arable paths in this intensively farmed area. Micklebarrow Hill affords fine views over the Trent valley.

Distance: 5 miles

Time: 2.5 hours

Start: French Horn, Upton, map reference SK 738544

Maps: Pathfinder SK 65/75 (Newark West), Landranger 120 (Mansfield & the Dukeries)

How to Get There:

By Car: Upton is on the A612 between Newark and Southwell

By Bus: Sketchy service between Newark and Mansfield

Refreshments: French Horn, Upton

Nearest Tourist Information: The Ossington, Beastmarket Hill, Newark, Tel 0636 78962

Go down the hill behind the French Horn car park and along a ginnel on the right: turn right in the cul-de-sac, then left after 25 yards along another ginnel to Church Lane. Turn left, then right to pass through the churchyard.

In a splendid setting at the end of Church Lane and on the edge of open countryside, Saint Peter's church's nine pinnacles are a landmark for miles around. Its tower holds not only four bells, but also a dovecote.

Turn left along the edge of the churchyard to a stile and follow the hedge right, crossing a footbridge, to Church Meadow Lane. Here leave the Trent Valley Way, turn right to the end of the lane, right to the main road and cross half-left to the footpath left of Millview Cottage. Pass through a gate ahead and up an old green lane to a stile. Turn left along the edge of a field. Go through the gap and turn right up the field and along the top to a double stile. Cross and turn left along the hedge to a stile, then right to follow the edge of two fields to a lane. To your left there is a fine view of Southwell Minster.

Turn right to reach a road: go right for 100 yards, then left diagonally across a field. Climb the stile and turn left in the garden, then left again through a gate.

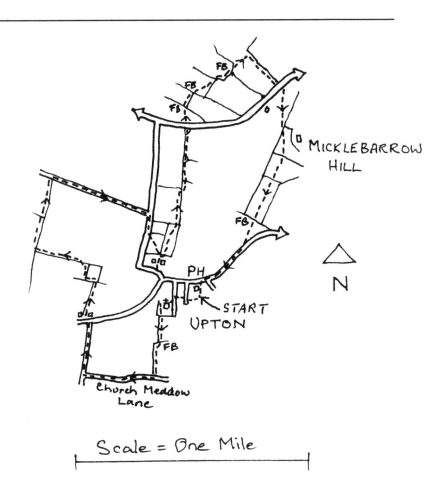

You are nearly back in Upton at this point and could halve the walk by crossing the garden, continuing down a drive and turning left to the main street. Continuing the main walk, a few steps right is a stile: cross the paddock to another. Now angle right to the stile in the corner and go along the edge of two fields. Cross the ditchboard and stile right, then turn left to follow the hedge, passing along the fringe of a small copse and beside another field. Cross a ditchboard to reach the A617 and cross carefully to the stile opposite. Go straight across two grass fields, then in the third angle right to Spring Wood. Follow the edge of the wood to the end, where a stile leads to a footbridge over a deep dyke. Cross and turn left to pass two electricity poles. At the hedge turn right and cross the bridge to reach the A617 again. Cross and turn left to a stile. Climb Micklebarrow Hill angling right, cross a stile into a paddock and follow the power lines to another stile.

Go down the hill towards Upton, go through a gate, straight down the next field, cross a bridge and aim for a pylon leftish to bring you to a gate. Turn right to return to your starting point for a well deserved drink.

28: KELHAM HILLS

A ramble on field paths and farm lanes just a mile or so outside Newark, with views over the Trent valley

Distance: 6 miles

Time: 2.5 hours

Start: Kelham Hall, map reference SK 774556

Maps: Pathfinder SK 65/75 (Newark West), Landranger 120 (Mansfield and the Dukeries)

How to Get There:

By Car: From Newark or Mansfield by the A617

By Bus: Regular services from Mansfield, Nottingham and Newark, few and far between on Sundays

Refreshments: Fox, Kelham

Nearest Tourist Information: The Ossington, Beastmarket Hill, Newark, Tel 0636 78962

A tiny village on the banks of the Trent, Kelham is dominated by the massive red-brick Gothick pile of Kelham Hall, built by Sir George Gilbert Scott between 1859 and 1862 for the Manners-Sutton family. In 1903 the Society of the Sacred Mission turned it into a theological college: it is they who built the Dome, which is such a prominent feature, as their chapel.

When the Society, for reasons beyond comprehension, migrated to Milton Keynes, the District Council made the house their headquarters. Both house and grounds are an attractive sight, as are the little church and the cricket pitch near the Hall.

Starting at the Hall, follow the path past the Dome to a little gate beside the lodge. Cross the road and go along the road opposite as far as the

South Muskham road. Here turn left, pass through the gate and go straight ahead across the field, passing a tree en route, and through a gate to a narrow road. Turn left, go round the double bend and through the signposted gate on the right.

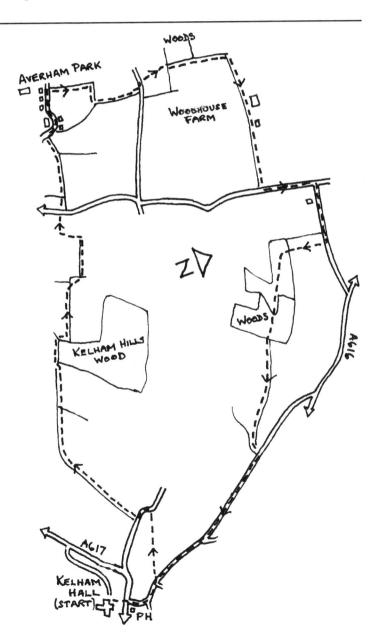

Follow the track, but where it veers left continue to follow the hedge to the corner of Kelham Hills Wood. You are now following the Trent Valley Way, and may see its symbol, a wavy blue arrow, from time to time. Pass through the handgate and along the edge of the wood. Cross a fence and narrow ditch, then go round the right-hand edge of the first field, slip right and go round the corner of the adjacent field to join a track. Follow the farm track to the road.

A signpost and bridge opposite take you across a narrow spinney. Go across the field beyond, with a wire and post fence on your right, then along a short hedged lane to reach a farm road. Turn right and follow the lane round between the old forge and some chicken sheds, then past a row of cottages. After the last cottage, leave the Trent Valley Way and turn right along the edge of a field, then along the far side. Here turn left along the field edge to a road.

Turn left for a few yards, then right and across a field to the corner of Muskham Wood. Only two edges of the wood remain, the rest being converted to arable in the 70's. Continue ahead past the wood and along

Kelham Hall

the fence to a stile. Cross and turn right to pass Woodhouse Farm and on to the road. Turn left, then first right, past the isolated Cold Harbour Farm and on to a gate set back from the road on the right. Follow the track down the field and pass through the gate. Just to the right are the ruins of a house and in front, two aged oaks stand at the head of a delightful valley. Walk down the dell, keeping just to the right of a tongue of woodland to reach a stile. Pass through the little wood, crossing a track midway, and cross another stile. You now walk down the edge of a meadow, then an arable field, rounding the bushes at the end to angle left to the gate. Turn right down the hill and continue to your starting point.

29: FARNDON

A very popular riverside walk. Most week-ends find boaters, fishermen and strollers enjoying the river Trent in some numbers.

Distance: 4.25 miles

Time: 2 hours

Start: The "Lazy Otter", Farndon, map reference SK 768522

Maps: Pathfinder Sk 65/75 (Newark West), Landranger 120 (Mansfield & the Dukeries)

How to Get There:

By Car: Farndon is about a mile south of Newark on the A46 (Fosse Way)

By Bus: Regular services from Nottingham and very frequent from Newark

Refreshments: Lazy Otter and Travellers' Rest, Farndon

Nearest Tourist Information: The Ossington, Beastmarket Hill, Newark, Tel 0636 78962

Farndon is a large village very close to Newark but determined to preserve its own identity and character. Its centre is the old village at the southern end, close to the river Trent. Here can be found a pub, a restaurant, a sailing club, the headquarters of a lively Sea Scout troop, and a busy marina.

From the Lazy Otter, walk to the right along the river bank past the picnic site. After the Scout headquarters, cross Farndon Harbour bridge and continue past overgrown gravel pits, then arable fields. On the opposite bank can be seen Staythorpe power station, now a shadow of its former self without its cooling towers. Just beyond this, the river divides into two branches, one tumbling over a weir and flowing past Averham, Kelham and South Muskham before rejoining the navigable branch. Herons and other birds can often be seen fishing on the weir. We follow the main river, which was canalised through Newark in the 1770's. Averham church can be seen to the left and the tall spire of the church of Saint Mary Magdalen, Newark is ahead. As we near the four-storey tower of Farndon Mill, there is a suitable path to the right to shorten the walk. This crosses the grass field past a fishermen's car park to a stile, then continues through two similar fields to join Long Lane and the longer walk.

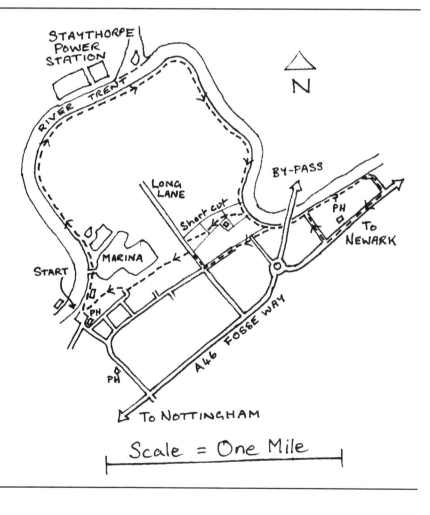

Scale = One Mile

Continue to follow the river past the mill and under the new A46 by-pass. On the right will be seen an old maltings, then some riverside houses whose gardens lie across the path. Unfortunately, the riverside path goes no further and we must swing right along Dorner Avenue to the Fosse Way. At this point the old Roman road has become relatively quiet as through traffic between Leicester and Lincoln by-passes Newark. The by-pass was opened on 4th October 1990. Turn right, and after passing the Travellers Rest and a row of houses turn right again down a stony lane past the ruins of old maltings to the river.

Turn left and take the narrow hedged path left past the mill, crossing a farm-track and continuing to join Marsh Lane. On reaching a mini-roundabout at a crossroad, turn right on Long Lane, then left after 150 yards. The track becomes a wide grassy path between gardens and the marina, which narrows to pass between garages. Here do not go on along North End, but turn right, then left through a glade of trees to return to your starting point.

30: SYERSTON

A short stroll starting from a Victorian mansion and featuring a delightful village.

Distance: 4.3 miles

Time: 2 hours

Start: Elston Towers (Coeur de Lion restaurant), map reference SK 747484

Maps: Pathfinder SK 64/74 (Carlton & Elston), Landranger 129 (Nottingham & Loughborough)

How to Get There:

By Car: Elston Towers is just off the A46 Fosse Way, 5 miles South of Newark, and is well signposted as the Coeur de Lion restaurant.

By Bus: There are regular bus services between Newark and Nottingham.

Refreshments: Coeur de Lion

Nearest Tourist Information: The Ossington, Beastmarket Hill, Newark (Opposite the castle) Tel 0636 78962

Start the walk at Elston Towers, an imposing Victorian mansion which, after a chequered career, has become a successful restaurant. On leaving the grounds, turn right to walk towards Elston. At the end of the first field, cross the concrete bridge on the right. Follow the hedge to the end, then go left for 100 yards. Now pass through the hedge right and follow the hedge on your left, approaching the village of Syerston. Cross a piece of uncultivated ground and pass a field grazed by goats and an elderly gander. The tree-shaded cottage behind the church is the Post Office. Continue to the village street, turn right for a few yards in front of the church, then left to enter the drive leading to Croft House. Just before the house cross the stile left, go to the far right-hand corner of the field, through a gate and along a short lane to Hawksworth Road.

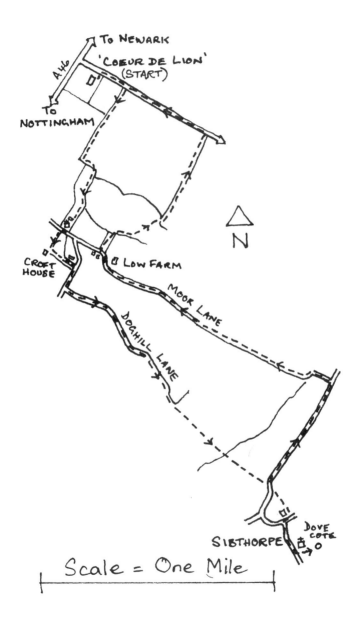

Turn right, then left along Doghill Lane, a pleasant hedged green lane with no hill to justify its name. When the lane ends continue across a field, a ditch and another field aiming slightly left of the nearest pylon. Turn left, which brings you to a road beside a footpath sign.

Syerston Church

At this point a small detour is possible to the tiny village of Sibthorpe, following a footpath straight ahead. A mediaeval dovecote stands forlornly in the field behind the church, and visitors are permitted as long as they leave things as they find them and particularly close the gate. The main walk turns left to follow the road as far as a track on the left just after a brick bridge. Keep left along the edge of a field on a bridleway which eventually becomes Moor Lane. This enters Syerston with a double bend: cross the stile right at the second bend, cross the field to the gateway opposite and turn right along the field edge. (It is proposed to divert this path slightly: any diversion will be clearly signposted).

Cross the field as signposted, pass into the next field and turn left. Go straight on, with the hedge first on your left, then on your right, to the road. Turn left and return to Elston Towers.

31: NEWARK TOWN TRAIL

People who live in Newark-on-Trent get used to explaining where it is: half-way between Nottingham and Lincoln is the simplest explanation. In fact it lies at the junction of the London to Edinburgh and Nottingham to Lincoln railways, at the crossroads of the A1 and A46 (also known as the Fosse Way), and beside the river Trent. It has played a major role in trade and in history, beside which it is a very attractive place to live in, and to visit.

Newark Market Place from the Town Hall

What better place to start than the Ossington. The Ossington Coffee Palace was built in 1882 by the Viscountess Ossington as a Temperance Hotel, to wean the populace away from the Demon Drink. This did not work, and indeed this magnificent monstrosity is now a hotel and restaurant. The Tourist Offices are in outbuildings up the hill.

As you walk up Beastmarket Hill, you will see two of the coaching inns for which Newark was famous. The Royal Oak and the Ram are both

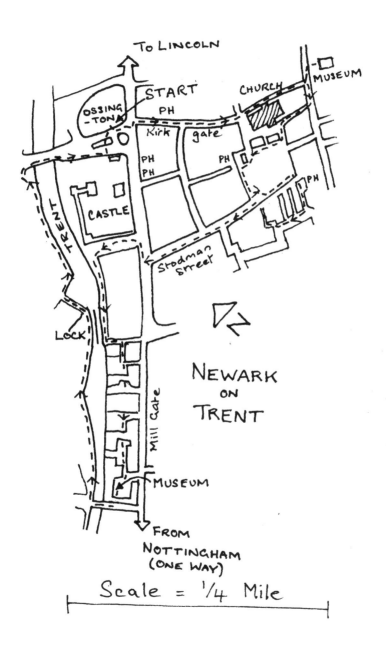

eighteenth century but very different in scale. Cross the pedestrian crossing and keep left, then right to enter Kirkgate.

You will soon pass the Old King's Arms, an early eighteenth century building which recently reopened as a public house with quite a range of draught beers. Over the door are the eponymous arms, in painted cast iron, of the Old King, George IV. The plasterwork 'Boar's Head' sign opposite does not indicate a pub: it was done in 1882 during rebuilding.

The view you now see up Kirkgate has often been sketched, painted and photographed through the years. At the junction with Middlegate is a fine half-timbered building, while nearly opposite are two more. The first one you reach (now offering Cuisine Française) has a plaque explaining that Queen Henrietta Maria stayed here during the Civil War. Her hostess was Lady Frances Leake, wife of one of the Royalist commanders during the seige.

Newark was beseiged three times by Cromwell and his Scottish allies, and the earthworks thrown up by both sides can be seen all around the town. It was never captured, but surrendered in 1646 when Charles I surrendered to the Scots army encamped outside the town.

Next to this 17th century house is a 16th century one, and beside this is the Italianate Old Westminster Bank, now a school of violin making, the only one in the country and part of Newark and Sherwood College. In front of you is the church of Saint Mary Magdalen, whose 237-foot spire can be seen for miles around. Built during the 13th century, it holds much of interest, notably the 'Fleming Brass', commemorating Alan Fleming, who died in 1363: it is one of the largest funereal brasses in England. Guide books are available in the church.

Pass the end of Wilson Street, a piece of eighteenth century spec building by vicar and entrepreneur Dr. Bernard Wilson, and continue past the Song School and along Church Walk. The churchyard has become a park, with the headstones tucked away along the edges. When you reach Appletongate, the Museum is just across the road to the left. The main part of the museum is a brick schoolroom, once part of the Magnus School, but more attractive is the original sixteenth century schoolhouse, built by the generosity of Archdeacon Thomas Magnus, and known as the Tudor Hall. Whether the large extension built in front of the Hall in 1817 enhances it is debatable.

Newark Market Place and Church of St Mary Magdalen

Leaving the museum, pass the east end of the church and turn right along the southern Church Walk, then left into the Market Place. The tall chimney behind the Wing Tavern is not an old brew-house, but part of the church's heating system. Much has been written of the beauty and proportions of the square, its arcades and the rich variety of its buildings. A fair amount of ink has also been spilled about its cobbles, many of which appear to have been laid upside-down by cowboy cobble-fitters. Fortunately, paving has now replaced the cobbles in the aisles between market stalls.

Millgate Museum

The building on the corner on your left, the Bacon Shop, now houses that *rara avis*, a good old-fashioned grocery shop, but once contained a printing firm called Ridge's. Here were published the first poems of George, Lord Byron, 'Hours of Idleness' and 'Fugitive Pieces', in 1806-7. For a tour of the Market Place, turn right.

Curry's is housed in a modern replica of the 1708 Moot Hall, the centre of civic life before the Town Hall was built. Angle left past the building society: beside it can be found the Pump, bearing the town crest, and the Bear Baiting Post. Slightly more puzzling than why bears were baited is why anyone would build this facsimile.

In the corner of the square is the timber framed Queen's Head, one of the town's many long-established pubs. This one dates from the early sixteenth century. Continuing our circuit of the market-place, we pass the Town Hall, built in 1773 by John Carr in the Palladian style. As well as an Adam-style ballroom, offices and dignified municipal rooms, the Town Hall once sheltered the Butter Market, an Aladdin's cave of traders' stalls, but it has now been converted into an up-market shopping arcade.

Crossing to the third side of the square we find, in a row of elegant facades, three former inns. The most imposing, the Clinton Arms, was Newark's top coaching inn, and under various names an inn stood on this site since 1494. Clinton is a family name of the Dukes of Newcastle, who virtually owned Newark. Distinguished guests included Byron, the Duke of Wellington and W.E. Gladstone, who delivered his election address from his window. Being the Duke of Newcastle's man, he was elected, several times. The building will soon be converted into shops unless someone saves it. The adjacent Saracen's Head, now a bank and travel bureau, was also an old-established inn, last rebuilt in 1721. It closed its doors in 1959, and only the bust of the Saracen's head remains. Walter Scott must have enjoyed his stay there, as he wrote it into 'The Heart of Midlothian'.

In the corner of the square is the fifteenth century White Hart Hotel, an ornate timber-framed house beautifully restored by the Nottingham Building Society which now lives there. Walk through the carriage-entrance, passing the present White Hart and a whole range of timber-framed outbuildings of the original inn, now being plastered over to create more shops. Keep right for a glimpse of the St. Mark's Precinct, a modern development which sits well with its historic neighbours.

If you take the third turning right, you will return to the market place near the Governor's House, which is on your left. The Governor in question, Sir Richard Willis, lived in this sixteenth century house during the Civil War: it has now been tastefully adapted as a cafe and bakery.

Continue along Stodman Street, passing the fifteenth century Woolpack Inn, whose timbers are hidden behind a plaster shell. A traffic island offers you a fighting chance of crossing Castlegate to the Corn Exchange, a Victorian monument to Newark's past glories. Corn is still grown, but bought and sold in less grand surroundings. Turn right, then left down a path following the castle wall to Cuckstool Wharf where, it is said, scolding women were ducked in the Trent. Apparently there were no scolding men.

Walk past Trent Lock and turn left just past Lock Cottage up a narrow ginnel. Half way up turn right to follow the Riverside Walk, which winds its way among renovated industrial buildings and smart new housing, as far as the old 'Trent Navigation' warehouse.

The warehouse has been converted into workshops for various craftsmen and a Museum of Social and Folk Life which vividly illustrates the lives of past craftsmen, their families and even their toys. There is a re-created Edwardian street, with shops, homes and even a bar. However the latter is only make believe, and outside in the corner of the yard is the 'Brasserie' where real food and drink are available.

Coming out of the museum, turn right through an archway and cross the bridge over the Trent, with a good view of the warehouses across the river. As you cross the Mill Bridge, to the left is a bridge over the weir which carries the river around Town Lock: beside it can be seen traces of

The Basin from Mill Bridge

one of Newark's many water-mills. Just ahead, you will find clear remains óf a much bigger milling complex. Turn right and walk past the Lock and Waterways Board repair yard, with a fine view of the curtain wall of Newark Castle across the river.

Cross the footbridge and walk beside the Trent. The door you see at ground level in the castle wall leads into the Undercroft, its storage area beneath the Great Hall. Only the pointed windows and the oriel window displaying the arms of bishop Thomas Scot testify to the remodelling of the castle in the seventeenth century. The castle is now being painstakingly renovated, so far a fifteen-year job.

After crossing Trent Bridge to your starting point, you could get a leaflet from the Tourist office and take a closer look at the castle.

Boot Notes . . .

CUSTOMER QUESTIONNAIRE

Please take a few moments to complete this questionnaire – you'll help us a lot, and you might win yourself a bottle of bubbly!

1 a Is this your first purchase of a Sigma Leisure book? YES☐ NO☐

b If no, how many Sigma Leisure books have you purchased before? ☐

2 Please indicate your **main** reason for purchasing this book:

a   for use with an Ordnance Survey map
b   as an alternative to a map for use on walks
c   for reference to local features of interest only
d   as a souvenir of a holiday
e   as a gift
f   other, please specify

3 Tick **three** main reasons why you selected this particular book:

a   price
b   cover design
c   presentation
d   content
e   recommended by a friend
f   assistance given in the shop
g   author
h   quality of information
i   illustrations
j   other, please specify

4 Do you think this book is:

a   good value for money
b   fair value for money
c   poor value for money

Continued overleaf . . .

5 Which features of the book do you like most? Please list in order of priority, i.e. 1 to 9, 1 being the highest priority.

- a   binding
- b   layout
- c   illustrations/photographs
- d   cover design
- e   size
- f   detail of information
- g   easy to follow
- h   content
- i   other, please specify

6 Do you think the book can be improved in any of the following areas:

- a   binding
- b   layout
- c   cover design
- d   illustrations/photographs
- e   size
- f   detail of information
- g   ease of use
- h   content
- i   other, please specify

Any further comments:

Please return this questionnaire to: Sigma Press, 1 South Oak Lane, Wilmslow, Cheshire SK9 6AR. If you would like a copy of our catalogue plus the chance to win a bottle of champagne, please fill in your name and address, below. The first three names drawn out of the hat on 1st October 1991 win the bubbly!

Name:
Address: